BRINGING HOME THE WILD

Bringing Home *the* Wild

A Riparian Garden in a Southwest City

JULIET C. STROMBERG

THE UNIVERSITY OF
ARIZONA PRESS

TUCSON

The University of Arizona Press
www.uapress.arizona.edu

We respectfully acknowledge the University of Arizona is on the land and territories of Indigenous peoples. Today, Arizona is home to twenty-two federally recognized tribes, with Tucson being home to the O'odham and the Yaqui. Committed to diversity and inclusion, the University strives to build sustainable relationships with sovereign Native Nations and Indigenous communities through education offerings, partnerships, and community service.

ISBN-13: 978-0-8165-5027-2 (paperback)
ISBN-13: 978-0-8165-5028-9 (ebook)

Cover design by Leigh McDonald
Cover photo by Juliet C. Stromberg
Designed and typeset by Leigh McDonald in Adobe Jenson Pro 11/14 and Archetype (display)

Library of Congress Cataloging-in-Publication Data
Names: Stromberg, Juliet C., author.
Title: Bringing home the wild : a riparian garden in a southwest city / Juliet C. Stromberg.
Description: Tucson : University of Arizona Press, 2023. | Includes bibliographical references and index.
Identifiers: LCCN 2022051953 (print) | LCCN 2022051954 (ebook) | ISBN 9780816550272 (paperback) | ISBN 9780816550289 (ebook)
Subjects: LCSH: Gardening—Arizona—Phoenix. | Urban ecology (Biology)—Arizona—Phoenix. | Riparian ecology—Arizona—Phoenix.
Classification: LCC SB451.34.A6 S87 2023 (print) | LCC SB451.34.A6 (ebook) | DDC 635.09791/73—dc23/eng/20230412
LC record available at https://lccn.loc.gov/2022051953
LC ebook record available at https://lccn.loc.gov/2022051954

Printed in the United States of America
♾ This paper meets the requirements of ANSI/NISO Z39.48-1992 (Permanence of Paper).

Dedicated to Mary Rose Gray

CONTENTS

BRINGING HOME THE WILD

INTRODUCTION

Y OU, LIKE me, probably live in a city. Most of us do, these days.[1] Do you have a garden? Do you watch birds? Do you occasionally pick juicy fruit from your neighbor's tree, marvel at the pollinators, or pop under a leafy canopy to stay cool? There is so much life around us, and there could be more. I am a botanist, now retired, who descends from a long line of gardeners. In my professional life, at the university, I specialized within the fields of riparian plant ecology and restoration ecology. During research trips to rivers and canyons of the American Southwest, I fell in love with the riparian trees who grow there. But I was tiring of driving to them. I wanted this regional bounty closer to home, without having to set foot in car.

Two decades ago, after looking at house after house in the sprawling metropolis of Phoenix, my partner, Matt, and I settled on a patch of abandoned farmland with associated water rights. Riparian trees and shrubs once grew not far from our patch of city land but had long ago been cleared in the name of progress. Ecological restoration is glorified gardening, some say, and that holds a grain of truth. After we repaired the irrigation valves that connect us to the Salt River, the water began flowing, and my restoration gardening fingers surged back to life.

What follows is a chronicle of our adventure in urban gardening and, more broadly, of our efforts to build relationships with the inhabitants of the ecosystem of which we are a part. We asked, "If we plant it, will they come?" with respect to the animals, and the short answer is yes. But, as it turned out, we were not the only ones doing the planting (I'm looking at *you*, birds). In these chapters, you will meet the companions we planted as well as the wildlings—plant and animal—who arrived without our assistance.

You may deduce that our philosophy differs from some, and you would be correct. Some staunch advocates advise urban wildlife gardeners to remove the nonnatives who arrived on their own, while simultaneously asking us to unleash the *wild* in our backyards by *planting* the natives. Such inconsistency makes me cringe. As homage to the notion that cities are melting pots for humans *and* for the plants who came with us, as well as to the notion that humans are not all-knowing, our garden embodies the principal of inclusive biodiversity. Of course, what is a biodiverse patch of green to some is a weed-filled mess to others. Read on to hear how we navigated challenges imposed by the city inspector who looked askance at our "weed"-filled bounty.

Are you concerned about global loss of species? Are you worried about the changing climate? I am, and that is why I ask much of our garden. I have high expectations. Plant ecologists speak of community composition, structure, and function, terms which refer, loosely and respectively, to who is growing there, what they look like, and what they are doing. With respect to composition, the diversity of creatures in our ecosystem amazes me. The quantitative nature of a scientist is hard to repress and, if you read on, you will learn just how many species of plants, bees, beetles, birds, butterflies, dragonflies, fungi, mammals, reptiles, spiders, and true bugs arrived to share space with us on our four acres. After a lifetime of teaching about the loss of riparian habitat, decline of pollinators and songbirds, and extinction of species, it feels good to be doing *something* tangible to help local populations rebound.

As to function? The members of our plant community are busy. The inhabitants of our garden are multitaskers. First and foremost, they are *warriors* in the battle against the rapidly changing climate. They also function as ecotherapists, keeping us calm and joyful by regaling us with their sights and scents and keeping us excited for tomorrow because who knows what new creature we will meet or new behavior we will witness. Another benefit? They offer up their green selves to help educate conservation biology students who hunger for field knowledge—those who are book smart but experience-poor.

Importantly on the hierarchy of needs, the plants in our garden *feed* us. Coming from a long line of farmers and grocers, I have long dreamed of growing my own food. I am still dreaming. But our food forest, assisted by pollinators, predators, and decomposers, gives us some of the carbohydrates and proteins we need to engage in fun activities such as climbing into their limbs. Velvet mesquite (*Prosopis velutina*) is the main workhorse, feeding us as she has fed Indigenous cultures for millennia. Pomegranates (*Punica granatum*), date palms (*Phoenix dactylifera*), and many others help put a (small) dent in the trips to the grocery store and a (tiny) bulge in our waistlines.

"It's like walking through a portal," a young friend remarked as she passed through the front gate. But gardens and ecosystems do not exist in isolation. They are influenced by the landscape around them. Our garden—"the place with all the trees," exclaimed a neighbor—is part of the patchwork of green spaces that is South Phoenix. We feel lucky to live in an area rich in landscape and cultural diversity. A quick jaunt down the way brings us to a community garden, a cotton field, a worm farm, a horse farm, and, increasingly, suburbs with too-large-houses in too-small-yards devouring prime farmland soil. I bemoan this loss. By the time you reach the last chapter, I hope I have convinced you of the importance of creating and nurturing diverse green spaces in the city. I hope I have made the case that *you* are an important part of the ecosystem.

Do you get along well with your neighbors? Peacefully coexisting with *human* neighbors can be challenging enough. There is much bias to unlearn and fear to discard when it comes to peacefully coexisting with coyotes, snakes, flies, and others commonly viewed as pests. I hope the stories in this book encourage city-dwellers to deepen their relationships with their wild neighbors and to be more respectful of those within our ecological circle. While we are on the topic of respect, there is another theme that wends its way through the book. Like others of my era, being female—and a female scientist, at that—has had its challenges. The sociobiological habits within our own species need an upgrade. Female voices need to be heard, as do the voices of those who speak for the plants.

Like other plant biologists, I am concerned about the growing loss of botanical knowledge and the rise of *plant blindness*, a term that refers to the tendency of the human animal to overlook the green creatures who sustain us. Scientific studies are showing just how intelligent plants are, and how important they are to our well-being, but plants are increasingly ignored in school curricula. Plants play a critical role in shaping ecosystems and human cultures, yet many of us have become disconnected from the botanical world.[2] Pokémon characters are better known among children than are oak trees (*Quercus* sp.), these days, and this extinction of botanical knowledge is happening at a time when we perhaps need it most: our fossil-fueled food systems are unsustainable. Parts of the world are becoming unlivable as greenhouse gases drive chaotic climatic extremes. Levels of anxiety, depression, and anger are rising in the young and the old, particularly for those living in cities.[3] I hope my musings about plants such as elephant tree, whose leafy volatiles transport one to a place of peace, or sacred datura, whose floral fragrances makes you glad to be alive, inspire you to befriend a green creature. I hope my descriptions of Anna apple, whose fresh cider can leave you speechless, and of chinaberry and Fremont cottonwood, whose transpiration streams keeps us cool in the ratcheting summer heat, inspire you to learn more about ecology and botany.

Oh—a word of warning: if you aren't a fan of dog stories, drop the book, now. *Drop it!* Dogs (and cats) are part of the human entourage. Matt and I live with a pack of four, and they, like us, benefit from a wild garden in which they can dig, hunt, and forage to their heart's content. But, as territorial predators, they occasionally have conflicts with their undomesticated counterparts who are trying to survive in our cities. There are negotiations to be had and lessons to be shared. I hope you find our experiences helpful.

Finally, I offer an upfront apology for occasionally getting on my soapbox and holding forth with rants. Hopefully the hints of humor, as well as the photos of our garden and nearby green spaces, will help the medicine go down that much smoother. As you turn the pages and pass through the portal into our busy and bountiful riparian garden, I hope you are possessed of the desire to grow your own. If you are? Don't forget your gloves. The world can be a prickly place. Dig in.

I

ECOHYDROLOGY

POPULATING THE GARDEN

IF YOU PLANT IT . . .

"I CAN'T **DO** this anymore," I whined, as we cruised down the curvy road. Matt, like me, is in love with the birds and the plants (and the dogs). During the first years of our marriage, like many riparian dwellers themselves, we were migratory. Many a weekend found us tooling down an Arizona highway to conduct research at a field site or delight in the wildlife of the enchanting rivers and canyons of the American Southwest. But I was developing migration fatigue. A phobia of high-speed travel was creeping into my being. Hurtling at high speeds down highways was pushing my stress meter into the red zone and polluting the air to boot. After one hot drive home from the mountains, in which the truck windows were open the entire way, all three dogs having been thoroughly skunked, it was time to think about a lifestyle change. It was time to find a way to opt out of the weekend urban outmigration but still enjoy the creatures we loved.

We began to wonder . . . could we entice *them* to come to *us* rather than *us* to *them*? (Not necessarily skunks, although that did happen. This time we were prepared with buckets of baking soda and hydrogen peroxide in which to wash the stinky dogs.) We began to ponder . . . if we plant it, will they come? We checked out place after place in the far-flung corners of Phoenix and finally landed in a very old house situated north of South Mountain Park and south of the Salt River. The house was neglected and abandoned, and in need of renovation, but it sat on several acres of land. Land with water rights, fertile soil, and . . . a dying grove of citrus.

Within the discipline of botany, I specialized in plant ecology and restoration ecology. Repairing damaged ecosystems was a focus of my research and teaching. I had immersed myself in concepts such as ecosystem health, disturbance regimes, landscape dynamics, thresholds of change, and regeneration niches. Matt is the environmental historian, and somewhat of an activist one, at that, having transformed peoples' views within the nascent field of invasion biology through his talks and writings. Here was an opportunity to transform words into deeds. To practice what we preach. And to not drive so much!

We thought long and hard about this decision. Another "carrot" was the opportunity to grow our own food. At least some of it. My grandparents on both sides were grocers. One of their fathers had been a sodbuster in the Midwest prairies, laying claim to 160 acres of Kansas land and becoming a farmer at forty. They would be shocked to see the giant stores of today, with row upon row of packaged processed particles that bear little resemblance to the plants that produced them. I wanted to grow and eat *real* food, with a provenance easily traced. And there was one more enticement that clinched the decision to settle on this patch of land: an animal shelter, where I could reignite my passion for actual underdogs, was but a stone's throw away.

The citrus trees, when we moved in, were terminal. They had been left to die, their irrigation spigots shut tightly off. But the future loomed bright and green. We settled in to fix up the eighty-year-old house—Matt is a handyman wizard—and grow ourselves a garden. A food garden. A habitat garden. A riparian ecosystem garden! Gardening fingers, once activated, cannot be slowed down.

FREMONT COTTONWOOD: FROM DATA POINT
TO MATRIARCH

Our four-acre garden has become an oasis in the city. Yes, they came, in droves, to answer the question. We have no natural springs, but the irrigation valves, from a hydrologist's perspective, are functionally so: surface water gone subsurface, albeit in pipes, to reemerge at rocky fissures, the rock, in this case, being concrete. We inherited the physical array of the irrigation system from the citrus growers who came before. From above, the property looks like a large, green fork; landscape cutlery art, if you squint. Four tines of xeroriparian trees, desert ironwood (*Olneya tesota*) and blue palo verde (*Parkinsonia florida*) among them, run east to west, lining thin channels watered by bimonthly gushes. A rhythm of sorts. Downstream of the leakiest standpipe lies our broadleaf riparian forest, which includes a

FIGURE 1 Looking into the canopy of Fremont cottonwood (*Populus fremontii*). Photo by Julie Stromberg.

tiny patch of Fremont cottonwoods (*Populus fremontii*). Even when a neighbor irrigates, they get a little drink.

I knew the parents of these cottonwoods. They grew along the Salt River and were the source of the seeds that Crystal, an engaging and curious graduate student, collected for a greenhouse experiment.[1] My graduate students and I would routinely conduct experiments to supplement the observations we made while in the field and this one yielded information on the traits that allow riparian seedlings to withstand silt deposition from floods, which can be substantial in arid regions. The experiment helped us learn about the capacity of four different trees and shrubs to thrive in their extreme environment, but as is typical in the world of science, it left us with more questions than answers. One of these questions was an ethical one: "What to do with the survivors?"

Sadly, most of the seedlings went into the trash. ("Into the dumpster? That's where they tossed you?" I once asked a little brown dog at the shelter who had put a paw on my knee and gazed into my eyes to share her tale of woe. *Who would do such a thing?* Who, indeed.) In our new garden, I realized, we had room *and* water to save some of the discards and that is how three lucky cottonwoods made it into the truck.

Once home, the leafy girls waited for weeks by the side of our house before we found time to plant them. Academic life is busy! Papers must be published. Data must be analyzed. Each time I walked past them I could sense their roots straining to be out of the constraining pots and into the limitless soil. Now, decades later, they have developed into majestic ladies. Our matriarchs. Yes, they are all female, releasing their fluffy white seeds each spring.

I wonder, though. Why did I choose to rescue the cottonwoods and relegate the others to a less-compassionate fate? And, if we are pondering, why have Fremont cottonwoods, among dozens of riparian plants, become the poster-plant for southwestern river conservation? How did they attain membership in the club of charismatic megaflora, an elite group led locally by saguaro cacti? The answer must lie in some deep-rooted need for similarity and familiarity.

Consider our relationship with the animals of the world. The endangered animals that tug most strongly at our heartstrings, and our purse strings, are the ones who look most like us, as in bilaterally symmetric with forward-facing eyes (think: giant panda).[2] The dogs at shelters who are adopted most quickly are those we have bred to look more like our babies, with great big eyes (think: adorable puggle).[3] We like other animals more when they resemble us. That narcissistic dynamic extends, as well, to the plants.

FIGURE 2 Northern mockingbird and northern cardinal at the water drip. Photo by Matt Chew.

I know that I am drawn to the tall and stately cottonwoods partly because they are more like us than some. Like us, they live for about a century—our timelines are relatable. Like us, they look like giant broccoli sprigs (just seeing if you were paying attention). Like us, they come into life as either male or female, more or less. Dioecious, botanists call this; one house for each gender. But these similarities extend only so far. If I may digress, let me say that gender roles aren't as constraining for plants as they are for social primates. I am betting the female cottonwood trees didn't grow up believing males were better able to photosynthesize. I am betting they didn't take a lifetime to appreciate being born female, or pretend to be a boy, because it was clear even back then who had more freedom and respect. How can one hang upside down from the monkey bars in a dress? How can one thrive in math class while being ignored by the teacher?

Yes, I was a tomboy, a term that is a wink and a nod to the notion that gendered behavior is not as dichotomous as some would like, in the plant world as well as in ours.[4] I am betting the young female trees didn't dig their way through layers of systemic abuse to reclaim their self-esteem. Please don't bury us so deeply next time. We may not emerge. Finally, after a lifetime, I have become a voracious champion of females. I like the boy cottonwoods *almost* as much as the girls.

GOODDING'S WILLOW: FILLING ME WITH GRACE

Goodding's willow (*Salix gooddingii*) is a tall, graceful tree of the American Southwest, named after American botanist Leslie Goodding. She receives less attention than her cousin Fremont cottonwood, with whom she mingles, even though *she* is the one who often supports more of the insects that sustain the riparian birds we love.[5]

Matt, by my estimation, is a super-birder. When I walk with him in wild places, it is as if someone has turned up the lights and the volume, illuminating the bird life around us. In our own riparian patch, I would not even be aware of the presence of many birds if not for him. Orange-crowned warblers, green-tailed towhees, violet-green swallows . . . such a colorful array. The garden bird list, now, is 157 species strong. We see riparian birds, desert birds, and those classed as urban. Many breed in our garden, including the curve-billed thrashers who can be wary of people.[6] The rain crows, or yellow-billed cuckoos if you prefer, who once nested locally in the dense cottonwood growth along canals, have paid us a visit. Twenty years in, we are reaching some sort of asymptote. Each new bird species is a reason for celebration, including this one: "Julie, come look!" Matt called. "At the water drip!" I trotted out to the front porch and watched as a little brown bird darted from mesquite branch to sky, catching insects on the fly. Such masterful swoops! Could it really be? Indeed, it could. A southwestern willow flycatcher was in our thicket, refueling, en route to his breeding ground. This one, number 112 on the list, was federally endangered. Well, not him, hopefully, but the species to which he belongs.

Two decades ago, I served on a US Fish and Wildlife Service Recovery Team for these neotropical migrants. I helped write prescriptions for their recovery but had yet to meet one *quite* so up-close and personal. And there he was. In. Our. Yard. Yes, it was a he. His colors bespoke his truth. After his short stay at our place, I hope he attracted a mate and found a thicket of Goodding's willow and tamarisk (*Tamarix* sp.) in which to raise a family. After their babies fledged, I hope he had a safe journey back to Costa Rica or Guatemala or wherever he overwinters. I can only imagine how difficult life must be for a migrant.

Loss of habitat in their breeding ground and in their wintering area has taken a toll on many riparian birds, including these flycatchers.[7] So, too, has loss of stopover habitat. While on their long migrations, these birds require way stations. Steppingstones. Safe places, not too far apart, in which to eat, sleep, and drink. To *be* a steppingstone for this little bird, after writing in scientific reports about the need for such places, filled me full of willowy grace.

THE SOURCE RIVERS

KUI: JUSTIFYING THE WATER

"What an extravagant waste of water!" admonished a colleague, after hearing about our lifestyle. "As an ecologist in a dryland region, how do you justify its expense?" A fair question. During my early years in Phoenix, as I lectured about water conservation and tended my xeriscaped yard, I might have said the same. Yes, I agree, we should not be wasting water. We live in a desert. Water is a limiting resource. There are too many of us living here, and more arrive daily. The Salt River is impounded in multiple places, as is the Verde River. At Salt River Project's Granite Reef diversion dam the pooled water flows out of the streambed into canals tracing those built by Hohokam people a millennium ago. As riparian advocates in favor of in-stream flows, how do Matt and I justify our out-of-channel use? How can we flagrantly irrigate a multiacre garden during a drought? Why do we feel so entitled?

Because this was a riparian zone, once. Our patch of land was not *quite* in the floodplain—we are three miles from the channel of the constrained and channelized Salt River. But the pre-dam riparian zone wasn't *that* far away. The Salt River's floodplain was miles wide, Will Graf's studies show, and her channel moved wildly and extravagantly about, carving new pathways, before she was tamed.[8] The land now known as Phoenix was vegetated by forests of Fremont cottonwood and Goodding's willow and by woodlands of velvet mesquite, known as *kui* to the Akimel O'odham—the River People. "When Phoenix was laid out, there was an average of six huge mesquite trees to each city lot," proclaimed an article in 1938, with the vegetation in places being "too thick to be conquered."[9] Shrublands of desert saltbush (*Atriplex polycarpa*) and creosote (*Larrea tridentata*) were abundant, too, according to vegetation maps from the mid-1800s.[10]

Those acres of riparian vegetation are long gone. They were cleared to make way for farms and orchards and then houses and highways. The forests and shrublands sustained by the Salt River became carpets of edible plants from the Old World and New, and then expanses of Eurasian grasses dotted by trees shading houses. Many of the bosques that lined other regional rivers are gone too, having been cut for firewood, cleared for farmland, or deprived of the water that sustains them.[11] Matt and I are giving homes to the riparian birds and plants who lived here before. We are restoring a piece of the riparian past, and that requires water.

The Salt and Verde Rivers drain large watersheds. Snow and rain that fall on the White Mountains, Mazatzal Mountains, Sierra Ancha, and Mogollon Rim and spring flow that discharges from aquifers in the Chino Basin provide water for many out-of-channel users. Matt and I settled on agricultural land with attached water rights. If we opt not to use those rights, there is no guarantee the water will stay in the channel to feed the riparian plants.

Is any one use more justifiable than others? How much does one "get" for each drop? In plant physiological ecology, there is a concept called *water use efficiency*. It refers to the amount of biomass a green plant produces per unit of water taken in. This concept could be applied at the landscape scale, to refer to the "amount" of ecosystem goods and services a unit of vegetated land generates per unit of water applied.

In the lexicon of Salt River Project, a unit of water is the acre-foot: the volume of water that would cover an acre of land twelve inches deep. The industrial-scale farmers who remain in the Phoenix area are using their acre-feet to grow cotton (*Gossypium*), alfalfa (*Medicago sativa*), or sorghum to feed cows and the beefeaters among us. The Phoenix Parks and Recreation Department uses some of their water to grow shade trees to buffer the climate and provide relief from the heat, with an ambitious goal of covering 25 percent of the city with canopy.[12] Pollinator gardeners are using their water to generate, ahem, pollinators. A declining but still large share of Phoenicians use their allotment to grow fairways of Bermuda grass (*Cynodon dactylon*) and greens of rye grass (*Festuca perennis*) so that wealthy men can relax and stay physically fit. An acre-foot of water, at our place, provides all those functions and more: food, climate buffering, habitat support, mental and physical wellbeing, and education. Our (cocreated) oasis serves as example.

To that colleague who remarked on my lifestyle and asked me that question, I would say this: I appreciate your perspective, but there is a salient distinction to be made. We are *using* the Salt River's water, certainly. But we are not wasting it. We are putting it to good and beneficial use. If a research team, somewhere, feels up to calculating the ecosystem services derived per unit of irrigation water applied, I would be glad to offer up our parcel of land for comparison. It hosts an extravaganza of life.

THOSE WHO CAN, DO

"Those who can, do; those who can't, teach." I often heard my father joke about this phrase in our home. As I followed in his footsteps, I laughed it off, but it nagged at me. During my academic life, I wrote about riparian ecosystems and generated information to guide restoration actions. It was satisfying work. I felt useful. But in my readings and wanderings, I learned that ecosystem restoration is not always effective. It sometimes can be harmful.[13]

There are official riparian restoration projects in the Phoenix area. Expensive restorations have been undertaken along the Salt River, collaborations between cities and the US Army Corps of Engineers.[14] After first removing the barrels of DDT and other poisons left behind by past users, they recontoured the land using bulldozers but then added their own toxins in the form of herbicides to kill unwanted vegetation. They pumped groundwater into the channel, planted trees, and sowed seeds. A primary focus was on regrowing the cottonwood/willow forests in the channelized riverbed. Up on the extensive high floodplains and terraces, on which the velvet mesquite bosques once grew, concrete and asphalt prevail. Those areas remain urbanized. Cultivars of South American mesquites (*Prosopis alba, P. chilensis*) line the streets and dot the parks, as do Chinese elm (*Ulmus parvifolia*), Shamel ash (*Fraxinus uhdei*), and others, but do not form woodlands, per se.[15]

A part of me needed to *be* a restorationist and not just to write about it. A part of me needed to *be* a component of a local ecosystem, integrating myself into the land and the water and plants and integrating them into me. If I was to make the notion of trophic dynamics come personally alive, within this scorching subtropical climate, I wanted to do it in a bosque along a river. Since the bosques were gone, we had to grow one. Learning how to harvest mesquite pods, and when, and ingesting them into my being, is satisfying some elemental calling of my own agrarian roots. It is a good thing to *do*.

2

THE PRODUCERS

DANCE OF THE DISPERSERS

ELDERBERRY: A FEATHER IN HER CAP

I N THE words of ecologists, plant communities assemble. Many processes, including the dispersal of seeds, influence the assortment of plants that coexist in a particular place. I sometimes refer to this flow of seeds as the "dance of the chories," *chory* being Greek for disperse. In our garden, we were not the only ones doing the planting. Yes, we brought in our share, but we were but one of many vectors. In a nod to the notion that our species is not all-knowing, we share space with those who arrived without our assistance. On the spectrum from French formal to English landscape, our garden pushes the boundary.

The velvet mesquite we planted by the water drip became the local perch 'n' poop, if I may be so crude. It may have been a northern mockingbird, or perhaps a phainopepla, who dined on the blue elderberry (*Sambucus cerulea*) in a neighbor's yard, down the way, and then flew to our mesquite to use the facilities and have a drink. Ingest a fruit, alight on a branch, and excrete the seed: the ecological process of zoochory. Blue elderberry was not on our list of species-to-be-planted. I have yet to see her along the Salt River, my main

FIGURE 3 Phainopepla perching on tree branch and a gibbous moon. Photo by Matt Chew.

reference river for our de facto restoration project. But here she is. In abundance. We dance a quick two-step, to celebrate.

Cities have high potential to retain the local character of their avian assemblages, say urban ecologists.[1] Seedeaters and omnivores often thrive, though insect-eating birds can struggle. Urban birds are mostly undaunted by fences and roads and other barriers to movement, though many are harmed by the noise.[2] Cities can be loud: Orange-vested drillers wield jackhammers, bearded show-offs gun their engines, and wild-haired women yell "Be quiet!" Oops, that was me. When a loud truck rattles down our relatively quiet road, the startled birds at the water drip fly a loop before returning. Some adapt by singing at different times of the day or projecting more loudly, to be heard above the crowd.[3] Others, like American kestrels,

FIGURE 4 Blue Elderberry (*Sambucus cerulea*) in bloom. Photo by Julie Stromberg.

abandon their nestlings from the stress.[4] Thank goodness the city approved our request for speed bumps, to slow the noisy cars down.

White mulberry (*Morus alba*) and common lantana (*Lantana camara*) were among the other plants transported to our riparian land by hungry birds. I am grateful to the birds for helping create a leafy haven from the soaring heat. What a feather in their cap. I am not sure which bird, if any, can take credit for the unexpected arrival of annual sunflower (*Helianthus annuus*). Perhaps a lesser goldfinch dropped a seed while en route from the irrigation ditch down the way. It is delightful to watch the finches hang upside down in these tall annuals, doing what it takes to extract a nutritious seed. It is good to see the world from a different perspective every now and again. I like to hang upside down, too. Who will the birds bring in next? Who will be next in the "assembly" line? It likely will be some choice morsel from a neighbor's yard, so I hope the neighbors have good taste! I am hoping for a desert mistletoe (*Phoradendron californicum*). Their flowers smell like heaven, and their berries are one of phainopepla's favorite foods.[5] If you see one of these parasitic creatures growing in *your* tree? Please leave her for the birds.

WIRE LETTUCE: BLOWING IN THE WIND[6]

"She loves me, she loves me not." Did you ever play that game? Did you ever sit in a circle with schoolyard friends and pluck florets from daisies, to let the floral Fates divine your future? Ah, it brings back such fond memories . . . especially when the answer was *yes*. I wonder what the plants would hear if they asked such questions of us? In our oasis, we planted many we had already grown to love, while remaining open to the possibilities of the sweet unknown.

Wind was another star of the show. Three cheers for anemochory! Sweetbush (*Bebbia juncea*), hoary tansy aster (*Dieteria canescens*), and wire lettuce (*Stephanomeria pauciflora*), equipped as they are with feathery hairs, arrived in gusts of wind from the mother plants who line our roughly paved road. I don't dare weed out these perennial friends who grow, as well, along the local streams. I love their adventurous nature. They can grow where they want.

But wait, what's that smell? Luscious aromatic resins are wafting from my fingers to my nose as I type. They are from camphorweed (*Heterotheca subaxillaris*), a fecund daisy who delights in the moist, churned soil of gardens and farms. She is a gambler who hedges her bets with dimorphic seeds.[7] Two different shapes, two different outcomes. A good fit for life with unpredictable humans. The seeds in her central disk are explorers, with hairs to fly in the wind. Those on the outer ring, the ray flowers, play it safer. They drop to the ground, right by mom's side. Why take a chance somewhere else? Because ... because ... yes, I did it. I weeded out some of these resinous girls. I yanked you right out of the ground. I am sorry. "She loves me, she loves me not?" Ah, the game of life seemed simpler, back then.

SWEETBUSH: BURIED TREASURE

Sweetbush, despite her name, is one tough plant. I placed her, once upon an academic time, in a functional-type category that includes hardy shrubs capable of tolerating stress (from drought) and disturbance (from flood scour).[8] If resources are scarce, and someone upsets your equilibrium, it can be challenging to start over again. But she manages. Her leaves, so small as to hardly be recognized as such, allow her to capture carbon while preventing too much water from escaping her pores. Her flowers, all disk and no ray, give rise to dozens of wind-borne babies who will alight on their own patch of disturbed ground, wherever it may arise.

Sweetbush arrived unexpectedly in our garden, but I know her best from the dammed and diverted rivers nearby. A ~~pirate~~ graduate student named Jere toted her soil corer into the floodplain of the dry, diverted Agua Fria River and then hauled her ~~pilfered~~ legally collected bounty to a growth chamber to entice seedlings to grow. She did the same on a reference system, the Hassayampa, which is protected for its value as a free-flowing stream. Jere was digging for buried treasure—as in buried seeds—because she wanted to know how readily a diverted river could revegetate once the water was turned back on. Floodplain soil, in the dynamic world of desert rivers, contains seeds not just from members of the current plant community but from older ones, too. Soil seed banks are a window back in time—a community memory, of sorts—with seeds from each temporal phase of the plant community being buried by each new pulse of sediment.

In the greenhouse, Jere was delighted to see seedlings of desert annuals germinating from the top layer of soil collected under sweetbush: popcorn flower (*Cryptantha*), combseed (*Pectocarya*)![9] As she moved deeper into the soil—deeper into time—she found the gems of the wetland world. Scarlet toothcup (*Ammannia coccinea*)! Toad rush (*Juncus bufonius*)! It was deeply exciting to realize this buried treasure of seeds can persist even after decades of stream flow suppression. It is reassuring to know that these embryonic plants are waiting, patiently, still receptive to the triggers that whisper, "Wake up, it's time." Unlike me, who is waiting *im*patiently for the water managers to turn the spigot back on. Flow, river, *flow!*

Oh—and a bonus of the studies? A new term. We biologists love our jargon if few others do. After this experiment, too, we brought leftovers home to our garden. The deposited soil gave rise not just to seedlings but to a neologism: *epistechory*. A seed dispersed because of the quest for knowledge. You are welcome, logophiles. Go on, dance your way home to joy.

MAKING LISTS

TREE TOBACCO: DON'T ASTERISK ME[10]

I love to make lists. Creating order in a chaotic world, even if illusory, is calming. I maintain a list of the dogs I've walked at the shelter where I volunteer (6,111) and of the species we have documented in our ecosystem garden (760). The garden list is cataloged by taxonomic rank, and Matt and I engage, playfully, in class warfare. Who will win? Class Insecta is running neck and neck with the flowering plants, and—oh, look—counting that new hoverfly, they have taken the lead. Go, Team Arthropod! No, I'm not competitive, why do you ask?

Species richness is an evocative way to refer to the number of species in an area. I have not directly compared our species richness to that of the restored riparian patches on the nearby Salt River, but if this was a contest, and that was our metric of comparison, I bet we would win, with our entanglement of plantings and wildlings.[11]

"But how many are natives?" some might ask. In my academic life as a plant ecologist, I would meticulously track down the origin of each species at a study site, as best as one could, and attach a little asterisk, as was the done thing, to differentiate the "exotics" from the "natives." I didn't go as far as some conservation biologists who refused to even include the newcomers on their site lists. If I apply that asterisking technique in our garden, I find that about half of the species on the list evolved in the region in which we reside. In terms of biomass, though? The Sonoran Desert regionals are the clear "winners" by far.

"Does it really matter?" I might respond. This asterisking habit harkens back to Darwin's era and, I believe, has hardened into a burden.[12] "Is it native?" is often the first question a student asks about a plant they see in the field, distracting them from more pressing questions. Preoccupation with provenance, I believe, diverts conservationists, as well as gardeners, from critical issues. Think: climate change, food security, or extinction (and no, introduced plants are not the main cause or even the second; there are peer-reviewed papers if you wish to read for yourself).[13]

I was an enabler, I am sad to admit.[14] Yes, once upon a time, I was deep into the nativist movement. Like many in my field, I was firmly entrenched in the extremist belief that we should allow no creatures in "our" region other than those who could verify that their ancestors evolved here. Slowly, I dug my way out of that hole. I realized what a fraught proposition it is to accurately determine who came from where, and when, and how they have evolved and intermingled since. And the words of the botanist Sir Arthur Tansley reminded me that ecosystems are but mental isolates with no definite boundaries.[15] I learned first-hand through my own research, and from that of others, that place-of-origin does not map neatly onto functional capacity in our ever-changing world. The costs of "invasive aliens" have been oversold while their benefits have been overlooked.[16]

The hypocrisy began nagging at me, too. If one requires that all plants in a restored area or in one's garden be from the American Southwest, how can one justify eating Eurasian wheat (*Triticum aestivum*) or soya beans (*Glycine max*) that were grown who knows where? How can those of us, whose ancestors came from another continent not very long ago, live here ourselves? I am all for respecting the Indigenous inhabitants, but in a comprehensive-lifestyle way. If invader's guilt is wracking our being, let's not redirect it towards those green creatures who came with us as we traveled the globe.

One such asterisked plant who invited herself to our garden is tree tobacco (*Nicotiana glauca*). She is stunningly gorgeous—skin so glaucous and leaves so huge. Like other mothers of her flighty style—she is a pioneer who reproduces early and dies young—she endows her plentiful children with few resources. Their miniscule size allows the seeds to adhere to muddy bird toes and fly across the globe, or at least hopscotch their way to new lands. She feeds the birds, fixes carbon, and stabilizes soil, but is too prolific for some. Sometimes we penalize success. She has gone too far, some say. She did not stay in her place.

One of my summer projects, *many* moons ago, entailed pulling tree tobacco from land along the Salt River that was being restored. *Nicotiana glauca* had no "papers" to prove she belonged and was put on their "list." I recall getting dizzy as compounds from her ripped tissues infused onto mine, which may be what triggered me to stop in my tracks and wonder what I was doing. Following orders to kill creatures I barely knew. And what an impressive plant she is once you get to know her. In many locales, hummingbirds pollinate her flashy yellow flowers, but in some areas where they are not around? She adjusts her stigmas closer to her anthers and pollinates herself.[17] Who are we to stop her journey?

That moment began my shift away from native purism. In retrospect, I now think of myself as having been indoctrinated. I had learned, in texts and lectures, that exotic species were "bad," a condemnation that perhaps belongs in church (though that, too, is debatable) but certainly not in school. After propagating this notion myself for a while, doubts, like the green plants themselves, began to creep in. I began questioning the use of tribal, divisive terms such as *exotic* and *alien* that separate *us* from *them*. I regret my role in helping to propagate the fear and dislike of those who came from somewhere else.

Tree tobacco, welcome to our list.

SCARLET PIMPERNEL: MORE THAN A NOVEL

Weed is a funny word. The father of my friend Sam calls her a weed, jokingly. It's a backhanded compliment—a way of praising someone for their persistence while wishing they would go away. Ecologically, weediness refers to a suite of traits that allow plants to proliferate on disturbed ground, which is something our busy, geoperturbing species excels at creating. Weeds, sometimes called ruderals, are known for investing in reproductive structures at the expense of maintenance or defense; some produce thousands of tiny seeds that fly in the wind or wait in the soil, ready to replace mom in a heartbeat.

Desert broom (*Baccharis sarothroides*) is one of those pioneering "natives" who is a bit weedy. Give her some freshly cleared ground and some water, and she proliferates. Unfortunately, some of desert broom's floral parts make Matt sneeze. A lot. I spent hours weeding her out in the early days. Several other plants have similarly occupied my time and kept me limber and active, but let's, for now, step over the ones who are prickly and itchy and turn to those new arrivals who bring pure joy. What pleasure to find new populations of nonprickly plants who have naturalized broadly. I love these jaunty travelers. Because, truly, who is wilder than a weed?

Some worry that the arrival of a newcomer—a weed or a wildling—will mean the displacement of the old. Often, as conditions change, new arrivals increase in abundance and others decline. But, as plant ecologists will tell you, it is not always a zero-sum game. Few plant communities are saturated in species—there often is room for more. Plants are going extinct at the global scale as we destroy their habitat, but diversity is increasing at the regional scale as we shuffle the biota and create new habitats.[18] Many of the reported threats from "invasive" species to endangered ones were anecdotal in nature and have not held up under scrutiny.[19] There will be some local extirpations in response to the waves of newcomers, but "the most general broad-scale pattern is one of invasion and coexistence," reports Tom Stohlgren and his team.[20] We can cherish the long-timers—the "natives"—while also welcoming the new.

Such as scarlet pimpernel! You may be familiar with this tiny member of the primrose family, with the scientific name *Anagallis arvensis*, if you are an avid reader of historical fiction. The details of her flowers as revealed by a magnifying lens are exquisite. Another cosmopolitan cutie is henbit (*Lamium amplexicaule*), in the wonderful family of mints. She, like scarlet, hails from Eurasia and North Africa. Both germinated in our orchard a few years back, their seeds arriving, perhaps, in irrigation water (hurrah for hydrochory!). Both are self-pollinating, meaning that each plant can reproduce on her own, without a partner.[21] Even a single seed can form a new population. I love their self-sufficiency.

Some say a weed is a plant whose virtues we haven't yet discovered. It is, indeed, an uplifting exercise to seek out and assume the best in others. Rising to high expectations is preferable to falling to low ones. Creeping woodsorrel (*Oxalis corniculata*) is good for a tart nibble; common purslane (*Portulaca oleracea*) is so tasty she is in grocery stores; even tumbleweeds (*Salsola*) make good greens when harvested young. And, in defense of the word weed, "a plant growing where you don't want it" is clearly a value judgement, subjective and context-dependent. The term is not masquerading as a scientific concept like some newer terms for unwanted creatures are wont to do. Yes, I'm looking at you, i-word. Still, alternate terms are compelling: cosmopolitans, volunteers, spontaneous urban vegetation.[22]

Who will be next to show up and assist? So much fun to wait and see. I hope they aren't too prickly!

TUMBLEWEED: MAKING IT ON HER OWN

Like many, I have a love/hate relationship with some plants (and with a handful of people, too). And with this concept! Who wants to occasionally hate the one they love? Knowing that the circuitry in our brain that sparks these two extreme emotions overlaps is helpful in not feeling like a horrid person. Knowledge of one's operating system is key.

I was out running late one afternoon, with my pack of dogs, when a windstorm swirled up. Actually, it was one of those dust-filled haboobs that makes the news every now and then. Outflow gusts from thunderstorms are such a tease. As I hightailed it home, I was not only chewing on grit but being chased by a snarling pack of tumbleweeds. I may be embellishing. They have no teeth. But they do snap off at the base and roll in the wind, shedding spine-tipped bracts and seeds as they go. Ouch, I hate you! Yet love you so deeply it hurts.

Tumbleweed, in the *Salsola* genus, is one who overcame a large geographical barrier. This notorious and short-lived member of the Amaranth family arrived in North America some six generations ago, from our perspective, or some 150 generations ago, from hers. She tagged along with a friend on an ocean liner, comingling with flax seeds in loosely sorted bags, as the story goes. She does get around. In her new homeland, she is well-loved by some. Western pygmy blue butterflies (*Brephidium exilis*) find her chemicals as compelling as those in desert saltbrush and other local members of the Amaranth family. Sculptors find her boisterous balls entertaining to work with. Those who watched sit-coms in the 1970s would be thrilled by her capacity to "make it on her own," if reproducing without need for fungal or animal partners qualifies as such. Others though? They don't like her.

In a letter we received from the city several years back, one you may have received if you are in the wild-garden game, we were informed in no uncertain terms that we were in violation of policy. Those tumbleweeds and other "weeds" greater than eight inches? They must go! Harrumph. Weeds, indeed. After calming down, we explained, in a multipage missive, that included a long list, that the 250 or so plant species inside our fence and on our verge are members of our plant community, performing functions that we value. We pointed out that there were, in fact, no tumbleweeds on our verge, just someone who looked a bit like her. We named the offenders for which we have zero tolerance—*Be gone*, tumbleweed! *Expelliarmus*, puncture vine (*Tribulus terrestris*)!—and explained our criteria for removal, trying to educate. The city, to our amazed delight, rescinded the notice of violation. Like Ms. Tumbleweed, we overcame that barrier.

Whew. What an emotional ride.

3

THE POLLINATORS

THE HYMENOPTERANS

BUFFALO GOURD: FOLLOWING YOUR PARTNER

WOOHOO, A new bee species in the garden! It is thrilling to document a new occurrence and see our richness rise. But where did they come from? The neighbor's yard? The canal bank? I should hop on iNaturalist to see where others have documented this little Hymenopteran. Organisms—be they plants, animals, or fungi—are constantly on the move. I moved across a continent, skipping from East coast to West, and before that my ancestors crossed the seas. Migration is ongoing. Sometimes, when one moves, their partner follows.

During one research trip to the San Pedro River in southern Arizona, a place where I spent considerable time, I became enthralled by the sprawling vines of buffalo gourd (*Cucurbita foetidissimma*) who were staking out territory on the river terrace. I was determined to replicate that in our backyard. I went on a quest for seeds, found some at my friend Rita's native seed store, and now this viny girl has sprawled her way across our orchard. She is a tuberous perennial, which is fun to say. Her leaves appear in April, and each year the reach of her stems extends farther from her base. Her flowers appear soon after.

"Yes, that *must* be what they are," I said to myself, one morning in May. I took a quick peak inside her big yellow blossoms and began jumping up and down with joy. I do get excited. The flowers were a-buzz with bees. Bees with a schnoz! Or, at least, a strongly protruding clypeus. Genus *Eucera*, subgenus *Peponapis*, tribe *Eucerini*, subfamily *Apinae*, family *Apidae*. Specialists on flowers in the squash family. Squash flowers are amazing, so felty and fuzzy, the males separate from females, and are even more so when filled with squash bees. They are among the third of the bees and wasps in the Sonoran Desert bioregion who feed on just a few types of plants; they are oligolectic, in biology-speak.[1] Their selectivity is part of what makes them fun to find. Not that I have anything against the generalist feeders, like honeybees, mind you. "You do you," as they say.

While connected to the internet—the hive mind—I navigated to NatureServe Explorer, which assured me that *Peponapis pruinosa* is at Rank G5, meaning globally secure. That's good news, assuming that's truly the species we have—identifying bees to tribe is difficult enough. Not only are they secure but they have *expanded* their geographic range, reports Margarita López-Uribe and her colleagues. The bees engaged with the cucurbits who were being cultivated by Indigenous farmers in central and southern Mexico thousands of years ago, eventually moving all the way into Canada following other farmers and their squash.[2] They now occur far beyond the historic distribution of their wild floral host, the lovely buffalo gourd.

A bonus of that day in May? Squash bees, like squash flowers, take siestas. Later that morning, near noon, I gently folded back a corolla tip and saw five squash bees sleepily curled around the central column of fused stamens. *Swoon!* One of them was missing an antenna—maybe from a squabble—and I named him Eric. Eric the half-a-bee.

You are welcome, Monty Python enthusiasts. Life is a flying circus, full of the unexpected.

PALO VERDE: DECIDING WHEN TO BLOOM

Good botanist that I am, I am in tune with the phenology of the plants in my region. I know, more or less, who is going to bloom

FIGURE 5 Twenty-year-old blue palo verde (*Parkinsonia florida*). Photo by Julie Stromberg.

when (and sometimes, why). Anticipating the progression of blooms throughout the year is fun and engaging. Some plants rely on rainfall and temperature to decide when to bloom, but others, including foothills palo verde (*Parkinsonia microphylla*), are more predictable. She and her friend blue palo verde cover the desert with yellow blossoms each spring, taking their cue from the day length.[3] Right now, while staring into this electronic screen, transfixed, my photoreceptive eyes are feeding information on the changing day length to my circadian clock causing my glands to secrete more or less melatonin accordingly. The palo verde outside—I'm not sure what trees are outside your window, look if you can—is doing the same. No, not checking her screen, though she may be tracking newsworthy chemicals in the air. I mean she is tracking the duration of light with her own photoreceptive proteins.

It shouldn't have been surprising to realize that bees, too, cycle seasonally, assisted by their own endogenous biological clocks. When Dorothy exclaimed that, "People come and go so quickly here!" she may well have been referring to the comings and goings of the bees, and not to the dwellers of Oz. They keep appearing and disappearing, into their nests. There are so many bees in our garden! A whole new world for this botanist to explore. Cactus, carpenter, digger, leafcutter, long-horn, mason, mallow, masked, mining, munchkin (just kidding), Sonoran bumble, sunflower, sweat, honey, and wool carder bees, to name a few of the twenty-nine taxa we have documented so far. And thirty wasps, too, including the blue mud daubers (*Chalybion californicum*) who keep the black widow spiders (*Latrodectus*) in check. Tiny bees visit tiny flowers, and large bees visit the large ones. Wood-nesters coexist with soil-nesters; stem dwellers peek out of their elderberry homes to see who is bothering them now.[4]

Some of "our" bees overlap with those I have seen in the riparian corridor of the Salt River, a few miles north; others overlap with those of ephemeral streams and foothills of the desert preserve to the south. I don't know if any qualify as urban taxa, in the sense of being more abundant in cities than elsewhere, because studies on bees in cities are not abundant. Resources in cities are abundant, though, even for hymenopterans. Once, to my surprise, I encountered a large group of yellow-green sand wasps (tribe *Bembicini*) along the canal bank bordering a nearby alfalfa field. Accidental habitat creation! Eccentric lady lying on her belly taking pictures of the ground! Adaption to novel environments is ongoing, as documented by the growing number of urban ecologists who are asking interesting questions.[5]

It is indescribably lovely to visit a green patch—I seek them out, like a moth to a flame, see a bee or wasp I recognize, and be in tune

FIGURE 6 Urbane digger bee (*Anthophora urbana*) at golden dewdrops (*Duranta erecta*). Photo by Julie Stromberg.

with their comings and goings. Such a sense of place. It is wonderful to anticipate the arrival of the early-bird mining bees (*Andrena* spp.) and welcome them when spring arrives. Such a sense of time. Whether we be plant, mammal, or insect, whether we are deciding when to bloom, when to stock our larder, or when to emerge from our nest, we all need to predict the future.

I suppose I will eventually get a handle on the temporal pattens of more of the bees. Maybe. For now? I am content to fall in love with each new bee I identify. My current fave? California digger bees (*Anthophora californica*), and here is why. I love to watch dogs dig. Watching Chip's brown feet fly furiously, the dirt going every which way, and the intense look of concentration on his face, makes me laugh with joy. As I laugh, he digs faster, which makes me laugh even harder and makes him dig even faster. Digger bees, I have read, and just recently witnessed, begin excavating their burrows "Much the same way a dog digs with its front paws."[6] Imagine tiny bee feet, digging away. So much joy!

BUTTERFLIES AND BIRDS

LANTANA: FEEDING THE ROYALS

Many people garden for butterflies, and we are no exception. Butter-flies are known for being selective when it comes to laying their eggs, so we must cater to the needs of the leaf-munching caterpillars.[7] We planted pipevines (*Aristolochia*) for pipevine swallowtails (*Battus philenor*), passion vines (*Passiflora*) for fritillaries (*Dione vanillae*), and milkweeds (*Asclepias*) for monarchs (*Danaus plexipuus*). We did not plant the flame acanthus (*Anisacanthus quadrifidus*) specifically for the Texas crescents (*Anthanassa texana*), or the desert hack-berries (*Celtis ehrenbergiana*) for the American snouts (*Libytheana carinenta*), but they found their hosts anyway. Desert senna (*Senna covesii*), with her entourage of sleepy oranges (*Abaeis nicippe*) and cloudless sulphurs (*Phoebis sennae*), popped-and-dropped her seeds into our garden all by herself.

We can be a bit looser, phylogenetically, when it comes to feeding the nectar-sucking adults. Common lantana, in our irrigated garden, serves as lemonade stand for many butterflies as well as, potentially, a pollen source for at least one.[8] Despite being shallow-rooted, this sprawling vine from the American tropics keeps her nectar flowing all summer long, undeterred by the wicked heat.

Occasionally at lantana we see one of the celebrities of the but-terfly world—the monarch—but more often they turn out to be queens, who they closely resemble. In the front meadow, one day in June, I saw a dozen queens flying about and landing on lantana's wide platform to nectar. I was determined to distinguish the girls from the boys, having read they were sexually dimorphic, in biology-speak. Here is what I learned: if you Google the term "male queen," prepare to be surprised. You will see courtship displays "on steroids," as they say. To each their own! Matt's quick eye discerns the males at a glance, detecting the scent patches on their hind wings, the little sacs that are filled with pheromones. The boys release these scented

FIGURE 7 Queen butterfly (*Danaus gilippus*) nectaring at sunflower (*Helianthus annuus*). Photo by Julie Stromberg.

chemicals as part of their courtship ritual. They think they smell nice and hope the girls agree.

Afterward, it is entertaining to watch the female queen decide where to place her eggs. She is choosy when it comes to feeding the next generation. She uses odor receptors on her antennae to detect airborne chemicals unique to her host plants and then, after landing, refines her search using taste receptors on her toes. In our garden, the queens are reproducing prolifically thanks to an abundance of milkweeds in the genus *Funastrum*, who graciously planted themselves. The funky odor of these latex-filled vines transports me to the Grand Canyon, where I first met them, their smell reminding me of the highly seasoned packages of dehydrated food in my backpack. Interestingly enough, *Funastrum* seems not to provide food for caterpillars of the monarchs who deign only milkweeds in the *Asclepias* genera suitable for ones of their exalted status. I may be projecting.

But wait, what's this? The monarchs, those endangered North American stalwarts, while I was looking away, have become cosmopolitan. In their new lands across the globe, some are feeding not just on members of the milkweed family but on gentians.[9] Host plant–switching by insects in novelty-rich urban areas, or during climate-driven range-change, may be more common than once thought. (If you were writing with a pencil, say, you might switch to a pen or even a crayon if one became available.) Contemporary and rapid evolution in cities is ongoing, says Sarah Diamond, one of the ecologists who has embraced cities as legitimate realms of study rather than as "artificial environment to be avoided for research."[10] In some urban areas, including Davis, California, introduced plants have become primary hosts for butterflies, researchers report.[11] From the point of "view" of the butterfly? So long as the chemical compounds she seeks are present, she will lay her eggs, regardless of the genus or family in which we place it.

The ecological world is complex, ever-changing, and increasingly globally connected. I am grateful for butterfly gardeners who plant plants but remain daunted by this realization: if we can barely keep up on the knowledge of suitable hosts for a celebrity—for the cater-*pillars* of society—how can we possibly do so for the others? Queens and monarchs are but two of the thirty-nine species of butterflies we have seen in our rambunctious garden (go, Team Lepidoptera!) and these are but of a subset of the 250 or so that occur in the region. And, for every butterfly species there are suspected to be fifteen kinds of moth!

I wish more of our neighbors would plant gardens for animals. I wish the swaths of sod that pepper our cities would teem with life, hosting plants from many different families to sustain insects from many different genera. I say this partly out of selfishness. I want the babies of the butterflies in our garden to have homes to alight on, after they fly away on their royal wings.

PERUVIAN APPLE CACTUS: A PERCH FOR THE HUMMERS

Oh, the flashes of color from gorgets, in just the right light, as hummingbirds dart and maneuver: sparkly red from Anna's and iridescent purple from Costa's. The colors are not meant for me, but I am up on my ladder again, taking pictures of Peruvian apple cactus (*Cereus repandus*), accidentally immersed in their world. It is a trip to Wonderland, without the long lines.

Hummingbirds, though a treat for the eyes and a pollinator of flowers, are territorial beasts. Our garden hosts three breeding species, plus migrants. Resident males squabble for ownership of high-quality patches, such as the one west of the house where chuparosa (*Justicia californica*) scrambles high into apple cactus. Chuparosa's tubular orange-red corollas offer copious nectar within reach of the hummingbirds' very long tongues. The tall columns of apple cactus provide perches from which males can dive, to protect their turf. The birds love that patch of red.

Scientific understanding grows in fits and starts. It is a work in progress, as we build on, and sometimes challenge, the findings of those who came before. For years, it was thought that bees could not see red and that birds could not smell. Pollinator syndromes were described, outlining the floral traits which matched a flower to its pollinator: bird-pollinated flowers are red, tubular, nectar-rich, and scent-poor, bee-pollinated flowers are blue or yellow with odors and landing platforms, moth-pollinated flowers are white and emit strong odors at night, and so on and so forth. The reality, as we understand it today, is more nuanced. Generalist pollinators are more common than specialists. Plant-pollinator matches are not as fixed as once thought, though the construct remains useful as a starting point from which to dive into the deliciously complex and rule-bending world of plant-pollinator interaction webs.[12] Bees do perceive red, it turns out, and some birds do use olfactory cues. Brown-headed cowbirds smell like sugar cookies, says the author of *The Secret Perfume of Birds*.[13] There is much to learn.

I am grateful to the young scientists who peer with fresh eyes, darting from their offices to challenge the precepts of old, maneuvering their way to the top. They are as wild as they come.

4

TENDING THE GARDEN

PUTTING AWAY THE MOWER: ADVICE FROM AMY

MEXICAN PALO VERDE: PRUNING THE PRICKLES

L AST EVENING, while hovering over my social media feed, I alit on this article of advice: "More birds and bees, please! Twelve easy, expert ways to rewild your garden," written by a woman named Amy.[1] An easy read for my tired neurons. A quick scan affirmed that, yes, we have implemented many of the relevant steps: resist insecticides and herbicides—check! Plant for invertebrates—check. Plant caterpillar food, too—check. Embrace weeds—double check! Dig a pond—someday, maybe. Leave dead branches and piles of pruning. Oh, yeah. That's where I dipped my proboscis in more deeply. It spoke to me in the moment. I know piles about piles. I have been creating them all day.

Some days I simply cannot bring myself to weed or prune. The thought is too abhorrent. The shimmering life force of the plants is too strong to ignore. Other days? Out comes the pole saw. I, despite my gender, can be a perpetrator of violence in the garden. Mexican palo verde (*Parkinsonia aculeata*) in particular, with her fast-growing wood, keeps me busy severing dead branches and live ones, too, where they dangle over the trail. The thicket of Mexican palo verde provides homes for valley carpenter bees (*Xylocopa sonorina*) and food for migrating warblers but, ouch, her spines can draw blood. She must be pruned.

Trees grow so fast in our subtropical climate, especially when irrigated by river water, that it seems my life sometimes consists of creating piles, moving piles, and thinking about what to do with all the piles. If we were in an active river floodplain, I could watch, from a safe perch, as the floodwaters raged through and entrained the branches in their roiling waters, tumbling their tough vascular threads into finer bits, transforming twig into twiglet on the journey downstream.

But, alas, we live in the city and have no scouring floods. No physical agent of hydraulic disturbance. Just me and my clippers, and oh boy, if things work out, maybe a mechanical chipper to share with our neighbor. Meanwhile, I am scoring A+ in the class of piles, playing the ecological role of shredder. I loved learning about ecological shredders, but I didn't imagine that processing coarse organic matter would become my lifestyle.

FIGURE 8 A desert spiny lizard (*Sceloporus magister*) observing its surroundings. Photo by Matt Chew.

To what end, you might ask?   Well, let's ask Amy. Ah, yes, to make homes for our friends. Placing clipped stems on a compost heap or leaving them in piles to rot will "make a home for small mammals, amphibians, and invertebrates . . . just like in natural woodland," I read. Reptiles, too. The desert spiny lizards and western whiptails (*Aspidoscelis tigris*) love our piles. Amy helpfully added, "They could take months to break down, so you have to think carefully about where to leave them." Indeed. Think carefully about where to leave them. As in, *the city inspector won't be able to see the pile if I put it behind this clump of trees . . . so this seems like a good place?*

Perhaps not what Amy had in mind?

GETTING PARASITIC

"Oh my gosh! Where's my camera?" I tossed down my shears, sprinted to the house, grabbed my fanny pack, and ran back to the tree. "Yay, you are still there!" I had been pruning dead branches from a Mexican palo verde (more piles!) and had startled a black chalcid wasp in the middle of ovipositing (her, not me). She was using that long hypodermic of hers to inject an egg into a larva of one of the wood-boring beetles I had recently photographed. I whipped out my camera and stared her down. She was not pleased. What a face. Sorry!

Now, I can't get parasites out of my brain. Not literally, that would be no laughing matter, I would be severely ill. In our garden tally of invertebrate species, a surprisingly large number are parasites. There are wasps who parasitize beetle larvae and kleptoparasitic bees who lay their eggs in the nests of other bees; such a complex dance of life. This year, I saw more California digger-cuckoo bees (*Brachymelecta californica*) than California digger bees themselves, and they all were visiting flowers. Forty percent or more of animal species, globally, may be parasites, and more are discovered each year. Some ecologists suggest that high abundance of parasitic species can be used as an indicator of ecosystem health.[2] If so, our garden is feeling quite well.

FIGURE 9 Black chalcid wasp (*Acanthochalcis nigricans*) on dead branch of Mexican palo verde (*Parkisonia aculeata*), inserting her egg. Photo by Julie Stromberg.

Yet, that socially based "ick" factor about parasites remains. Some conservationists kill cowbirds because they lay their eggs in someone else's nest. Some pollinator gardeners dislike cuckoo bees because they do the same. We humans can be hypocritical though. As carnivores, and even as vegetarian herbivores, we can't claim much moral high ground. Oh, to be a self-sufficient autotroph, feeding directly from the sun, free of ethical quandaries.

Still, why does my empathy lie with the beetle? Yes, there is something off-putting about imagining oneself being slowly eaten alive, but in truth I have no idea what it is like to be a xylem-feeding beetle larva, parasitized or not. There is so much we don't know. Making decisions about what to protect and when to interfere in an ecosystem or habitat garden or someone else's life is fraught. Some gardeners kill caterpillars to protect their plants without considering the birds they are depriving of food; others try and protect monarch caterpillars by shooing the milkweed bugs (*Lygaeus kalmia, Oncopeltus fasciatus*) away. We act out of empathy and emotion, personal preferences, and ecological knowledge but really are clueless, flailing about in the dark like other organisms on this planet, no matter how many cells we have or how we obtain the nutrients and energy we need to make more of ourselves.

At the very least, let's give all the creatures in our garden the benefit of the doubt before *we* dive in for a kill. And whatever you may be doing, don't forget to smile for the camera. You never know who might be watching.

BLOOD SAGE: NO MOW MAY

To encourage more birds, bees, and butterflies, conservation gardeners (including Amy!) recommend changing your relationship with your lawnmower. Mow your lawn less frequently, or mow it in strips, because lawnmowers are violent, destructive, and noisy.

When I was a kid, I loved mowing lawns. Earn some pocket change, breathe in the sharp scent of fresh-cut grass, carefully follow the inward spirals and make rings around the trees; a good way to spend a Saturday morning after the cartoons had come and gone. But those scents—those green leaf volatiles?[3] They are the scents of distress.

Over the years, the size of the patch that we mow has shrunk in size. Our front yard is now a meadow, completely mower free. That decision was easy and gradual. Bermuda grass slowly gave way as the velvet mesquites cast more shade, and ceded to the equally rhizomatous Mexican evening primrose (*Oenothera speciosa*) and to waist-high blood sage (*Salvia coccinea*), an herbaceous perennial who decided she liked our soil and climate just fine, thank you very much. The primrose and sage are bordered by annual sunflowers, whose multistoried leaves provide stacks of transpirationally cooled apartments where insects seek shelter on very hot days.

In the orchard, we would occasionally mow strips to allow water and feet to move freely between basins. A few years ago, though, as I was mowing such a strip, I saw a large dark butterfly and quickly cut the motor. I slow-moseyed over to investigate. . . . "Wow, a dark

FIGURE 10 Mexican hat (*Ratabida columnifera*) in the unmown orchard. Photo by Julie Stromberg.

buckeye," I exclaimed. "Another yard first." They have patches on the wings that resemble seeds of Ohio buckeye (*Aesculus glabra*), a tree you may know from the Midwest. That "wow" was followed by another one, this one quieter and internal, as it dawned on me that the orchard, too, was morphing into a butterfly meadow. The fruit trees are widely spaced, and the sunny patches in between are filling with purple three awn (*Aristida purpurea*), Mexican hat (*Ratibida columnifera*), and other plants who feed insects.

Ah, the joy of setting aside one's expectations and letting events unfold. The joy of multifunctional landscapes. The joy of turning off the mower. Thank you, Amy, for your gardening advice!

PUTTING AWAY THE TOXINS

DOMESTICATED COTTON: BLUE SEEDS SEND A WARNING

There is a farm field across the street from us. It is owned by the city of Phoenix and leased to a farmer. The field in most years is planted with domesticated Mexican cotton (*Gossypium hirsutum*). This year is no exception, and there is row after row of genetically identical plants. The farmer cuts short the lives of these perennials in their youth to harvest their oil-rich seeds (to feed cows) and to harvest the fiber-filled fruits (to keep us clothed and bedded). The fibers are called staples, which sounds unpleasant to sleep on but isn't. In winter, the bare earth of the harvested field cries at me like an open wound. Raw. In need of healing cover. The tractors go back and forth, plowing deep, burning fuel, exposing soil to the wind. Our house is coated with dust.

We don't use toxins in our garden—no herbicides or insecticides or fungicides—but this farmer does. I walked across the street one spring morning to see if any of the bees who pollinate the trees in our orchard were spilling across to the cotton field. Yes, a few were, and I wished them well. As I looked down, I was distracted by bright patches of blue littering the ground. That looks wrong! The colors turned out to be the shed coats of the cotton seeds. They were as bright as the colors on the milkweed bugs who live in our garden and sequester poison from their host plants. The color on the cotton seeds, too, serves as warning. The dyes are applied by agro-industrial conglomerates, and they, similarly, declare, "Back off, lady." They may mean a seed has been coated with fungicides or insecticides, or that the baby plants have been genetically modified to survive future dousing with herbicides. "Yuck," I said, eloquently, as I tossed the blue coats back to the ground. So much poison. There are better ways.

When I got home, I washed my hands, as I was already feeling a tingling in my lips from the toxins. Farm workers and others get sick and die as their poisons spill over, onto us.[4] Many believe herbicides kill only plants, but that is not always the case. The poisons drift in the air and are carried away in the water, causing nontarget effects. Bees have their own lives cut short. I don't know what I can do to help them other than growing my own, shopping responsibly, and wearing my jeans until my bare knees poke through the withered staples. To protect myself from the toxins *and* the vehicular noise? I close the windows and find balls of cotton to stuff in my ears.

FLAX: PLOWING THE FIELDS

When I gaze at the cotton field across the way, and then glance down at my own jeans, I feel a tinge of guilt. But only a tinge. I am not one to overindulge in new clothes. On those blue-moon occasions when I dress in something other than cotton-based blue jeans and tee-shirts, recycled from the thrift store, I choose a garment made of linen. I like the way it feels. I also prefer the feel of a paper dollar in my hand to that of a plastic card. Fibers from the flax (*Linum*) plant, called linen, mingle with those from the cotton plant to give the US bill its soft crispness. Money may not grow on trees, but it does grow on herbaceous perennials.

I come from an upper middle-class background. My material needs were met and then some. Years after his death, the royalties from dad's professional writing trickled in, for which I remain grateful. Not having wanted for money allowed me the luxury of disliking it, or at least the consumerist, capitalist philosophy it represents. I am not a fan of the effects that industrial agriculture, as practiced in our country, has on our ecosystems, and the same goes for the effects of capitalism. Its false narrative force feeds us a false brand of happiness. You can't buy your way to joy.

Certainly, a threshold amount of money is essential to keep one fed, healthy, and educated. Beyond that? Consumptive luxury is a death sentence. "Making a killing on Wall Street" is too literally true for my tastes. My first inclination, after seeing an item advertised for sale, is to empathize with those creatures who lost their lives so that it could be produced. I ponder *who* was transformed into *what*. "The price of anything is the amount of life you exchange for it, immediately or in the long run" to paraphrase Henry David Thoreau.[5] Rather than adding another item to my wardrobe, I would be happier to have made the acquaintance of the green creatures who lived on the field before it was plowed for someone's pleasure.

I hope these sentiments don't offend. It's just the way I feel.

5

THE CONSUMERS

EATING LOCAL

SNATCHING THE BAGEL

"**S**CORE!" I snatched a whole bagel from the trashcan. I can't stand it when people waste food. "I hope no one was watching!" I was attending an event at an animal shelter near our house, while also looking out for my own pack. We have *only* four dogs, but that is many mouths to feed, explaining why I get excited when I find free food. (I *so* wanted a dog when I was young, but my brother was allergic. I am making up for lost time.) Feeding our active and adventurous pack requires considerable kibble to supplement their hunting of rabbits and foraging of fruit. Our living room carpet right now is littered with seeds of date palms, evidence of their latest afternoon snack.

As I was driving home from the bagel-snatching event, I saw a skinny Rottweiler at an overturned garbage can. She was scarfing down scraps. As I got out of the car to help (to help rescue, not to help scarf; I am not that feral yet), I pondered the bond between our two species. Food was at the root of our relationship with dogs and remains so today. Wolves hunted with our ancestors, warned them of danger, and scavenged in their waste piles. Our ancestors, in turn, played with their puppies and ate them during times of scarcity.

(Ew!) One does what one needs to survive, I suppose. A strong and enduring partnership ensued.[1]

Waste makes me fret, as does thinking about the systemic changes our society needs to make, soon, if we are to feed the eight billion of us, *and* our companion animals, without irreparably damaging our soils and our aboveground ecosystems, too. Not wasting food is one place to start. Going local, very local, is good, too. We, in our own four-acre patch of green, increasingly nibble off the land, feasting from the productivity of our deep, rich, alluvial Rillito loam. Prime farmland soil. I don't know if you have tried to feed yourself from your own garden, but if you have, or if you have read books such as *Animal, Vegetable, Mineral: A Year of Food Life*[2] or *Wild Idea: Buffalo and Family in a Difficult Land*,[3] you know how much effort goes into producing even a single grain of an edible grass.

If you are an urban farmer, I am guessing it wasn't you who tossed that bagel.

PARTITIONING THE RESOURCE

The coyotes were singing last night. Or maybe they were laughing. I like to think they were. I love to listen to them, despite the frisson of worry it brings. No, not worry about risks to our domesticated pack, but risks to the coyotes themselves. These wily canines are remarkably able to survive in our cities—the one who rides the tram in Portland, so worldly(!)—yet dangers lurk.[4]

Our own species is equally remarkable. We have transformed the planet, co-opting a lion's share of the land and fresh water, using much of it to grow food.[5] Croplands and pastures now rival forests in their spatial extent. Our global water footprint is large, leaving less for our wild neighbors.[6] They, increasingly, rely on our bounty.

Matt and I often see coyotes in the field that borders our city land to the south, though I wouldn't want to hunt in those chem-blasted rows. Beyond that lies a ridge of desert mountain. I mention these cardinal details because the matrix in which any patch of land is embedded is important. The matrix, as you may know if you have taken a course in Landscape Ecology, is more than a dystopian movie. The matrix is the prevalent, or background, land use. Conditions inside of a patch, even if that patch is fenced, are influenced by what happens outside of the patch. Energy flows and matter cycles—and sometimes, jumps fences.

Coyotes, enticed by scampering desert cottontails (*Sylvilagus audubonii*) and sweet pods of mesquite, easily jump into our irrigated oasis to hunt and forage. We are glad to share, but our dogs take a different view. When wild and domesticated nature come into proximity, the interactions can be X-rated. Coydogs happen. We haven't seen the sex, but we have seen the violence. If you were betting on the coyote, guess again. Our territorial dogs, sadly, have killed more than one coyote. Our oldest female, Sunshine, is the main huntress; we should have named her Athena. The others—all large breeds—are her support team. The deaths have been painful to witness. We lamented them with our own wild howls: *we must make changes!*

Co-existing with your neighbors, be they four-legged or two, is a challenge. Good ecologists that we are, we opted for the tried-and-true approach of divvying up the spatial resources in time. Ecological resource partitioning.[7] We summoned our inner masons to build a small fence and restricted the nighttime access of the dogs to the enclosed inner yard. The dogs have free rein in the outer yard during the day, and the coyotes have it at night. Seems to be working, for now. Paws crossed. All sixteen of them.

Coyote shares a name with a riparian shrub called coyote willow who grows along the local streams. She goes by the scientific name of *Salix exigua*. *Salix* derives from Celtic "sal" which means "near" and "lis" which mean "water"; her specific epithet *exigua* denotes small. Her diminutive leaves allow her to tolerate drier conditions than many willows. As to her common name? The dense thatch she sends up from her underground stems entices coyotes to bed down for the night. She, like her namesake, is a survivor in the Anthropocene. Singing her own song of truth.

I wonder if she, too, is laughing. I like to think she is.

LIVING IN A MESQUITE BOSQUE

VELVET MESQUITE: GOING DEEP

Some trees, when you first meet them, reveal only a part of themselves. Velvet mesquite is one such creature. She has depth to her character but hides much of who she is. Perhaps that is why I like her so very, very, much. I first became enamored when I learned, during my studies, that mesquite could grow her roots *way down* to the water table. Fifty meters. That's ten times longer than her trunk. A root-to-shoot ratio to envy. A botanist named Walter Phillips, decades ago, found roots at the base of an open pit mine and the anatomy of the tissue suggested they belonged to her.[8] She typically grows her roots shallower, tracking the water table but still in the record-setting realm.[9] Some of the deep-sourced water leaks from her tissues into shallow soil—hydraulic lift, this is called—benefiting those who are less radicle-endowed.[10] So much goes on beneath the surface, of which we are unaware.

Mesquite's productivity in our garden is enabled by water diverted from the Salt River. Water tables in parts of Phoenix, as in many desert cities, have been drawn down by electrically pumped wells, and groundwater is no longer accessible to even the deeply rooted. We, as a society, are not sharing very well. It is a good thing, then, that velvet mesquite is flexible. She also grows wide-spreading laterals, just below the soil surface, to capture water from rain or irrigation. The sound of the gentle trickle is delightful. Mesquite "hears" the water and grows toward it. Her underparts do, anyway. Acoustic gradients allow her to detect water sources from afar and moisture gradients then allow her to home in on her target more accurately, researchers say.[11] Mesquite's root hairs soak up the periodic flows, the irrigation water acting like clockwork flood.

My admiration for velvet mesquite increased after learning about her capacity to engage with tiny creatures who have mastered the miraculous feat of converting atmospheric nitrogen into ammonia.[12] Before she allows the nitrogen-fixing rhizobia into her body, they do a delicate, chemical, pas de deux. Are you friend or foe? Mutualist or pathogen? Her root tips secrete signaling chemicals into the soil, the bacteria "listen" and respond, and she completes the conversation. Nodulate away! Once in, she supplies her single-celled dwellers with the energy they need to drive the enzymatic catalysis. In exchange, they give her the nutrients she needs to create her protein-rich fruit. A fine partnership, indeed.

Mesquite's ability to obtain water and nitrogen where few others could allowed her to become abundant along rivers in the American Southwest. And she shares her bounty. Think McDonalds in the city, except nutritious and free. She packages the considerable carbon she fixes in hand-size morsels that feed us, the coyotes and round-tailed ground squirrels (*Xerospermophilus tereticaudus*) alike, so we overlook the occasional poke from her thorns.

Marcella, our young neighbor to the north, came over this morning to help harvest the pods. Marcella is sweet, just like them. She is learning to live off the land and has a garden of her own. We share food and local knowledge; it is nice. I hauled out the stepladders

FIGURE 11 Flowers and pollinators of velvet mesquite (*Prosopis velutina*). Photo by Julie Stromberg.

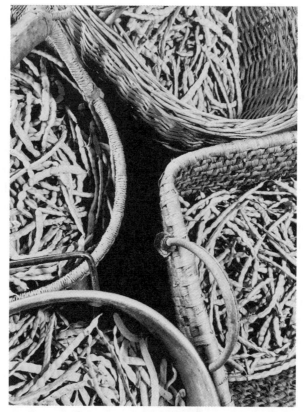

FIGURE 12 Harvested pods of velvet mesquite (*Prosopis velutina*). Photo by Matt Chew.

and we climbed into the canopy, picking the pods that were dry and leaving the ones that were still green, slowly filling our bags. Some velvet mesquite have long, thin, red-streaked pods while others are plumper and less colorful. Each is different. Matt is our sommelier, of sorts, tasting the pods and selecting the most delectable trees to harvest.

The community milling is but a few days away, during which the starchy pods will be transformed into flour and then into us. I cook with the flour throughout the year, tossing it into pancakes or crackers or, last night, apple-zucchini bread. Yum. A mini culture has resprung around this regionally important food which helps stabilize one's blood sugar while giving the bacteria in one's digestive tract something to do.[13] As we picked the pods up high, our huntress, ~~Athena~~ Sunshine, was down low, munching on her breakfast selection. Well done, you! Less kibble to buy from the store.

HONEY MESQUITE: CONNECTING WITH THE PAST

I am certainly not the only one to have decided that mesquite bosques are fine places to live.[14] The presence of groves of mesquite, be they honey (*Prosopis glandulosa*), screwbean (*P. pubescens*), or velvet, were determining factors in settlement location for many people of the American Southwest.

"Velvet mesquite was the tree of life, the principal food to the River Pima [Akimel O'odham]," writes Wendy Hodgson in her award-winning book.[15] Honey mesquite pods were a "staple of life" to the Mohave, Quechan, Cocopah, and Cahuilla people and ensured against starvation during years with scant rain. The pods were used for commerce, too: those who lived along the low desert rivers traded mesquite pods for acorns (*Quercus*) and piñon (*Pinus*) with those who lived in the highlands.

Despite being displaced from their ancestral homes, some American Indians continue to harvest mesquite today. Some harvest two crops per year, in late June and again in October. One member of the Akimel O'odham, as Wendy Hodgson notes, recalls families gathering in summer to collect two *wagon loads* of mesquite pods in a day. Reading such passages inspires me to ramp up our own harvest and turn it into a community event.

Our society has become complacent. It is *too* easy to obtain calorie-rich food in this modern era. Healthy people pay money to drive to the gym to turn wheels on bikes that go nowhere, and then pay more money to buy a quick meal of excess calories, perpetuating the cycle. We have outsourced our food production to others, fueled by external subsidies, in our specialized society, but there are risks in becoming too domesticated and too disconnected from our roots.

There is joy to be found in connecting with the past, filling our bellies with ancestral foods, and knowing the names of those who are being turned into us. You are, indeed, ~~what~~ who you eat.

NIBBLING AT THE EDGES

WILD LETTUCE: EXPERIENTIAL LEARNING

"It's following us! Look, it's dancing around our heads." I was in the mesquite-dotted orchard with a small group of students from Matt's field class in Novel Ecosystems. I was fielding their questions about all things botanical when an airborne seed of wild lettuce (*Lactuca serriola*) became caught in the eddies of our movements and began acting like part of our group. "You need a goat in here," exclaimed another student, as they moved through the undergrowth. They were an interesting bunch, as usual. Some were at home in the out-of-doors, having visited a grandparent's farm or been taken camping by their parents. Most were city kids, raised on a diet of mediated nature. But they all were hungry for knowledge.

FIGURE 13 Milkweed seeds in the wind. Photo by Julie Stromberg.

We began nibbling at the edges. We started with the legumes. There were four members of the *Fabaceae* nearby, two of them trees, one a vine, and the other a shrub. I asked the students to look closely to see what features they had in common. Being able to identify a plant to family is a useful way to orient oneself in an unfamiliar landscape. As they examined the shape of the leaves, flowers, and fruit, I plucked a purple flower from the sprawling corkscrew vine (*Cochliasanthus caracalla*) and asked, "Anyone want to taste this?" before popping one into my mouth. "They make an excellent coleslaw. Don't worry about the tiny ants who pollinate the flowers, they add a bit of zest."

Field classes are in crisis these days. The fields of ecology and conservation are relatively young—the journal *Ecology* was first published in 1920, *Conservation Biology* in 1987, and *Restoration Ecology* in 1993—and the student populations continue to grow.[16] But opportunities for outdoor experiences are declining. Field classes are by necessity small but class sizes at universities are increasing. Experiential learning is critical for ecologists and field biologists, as well as for novice farmers, but remote education is gaining sway. The written word is essential but insufficient: "Written texts transform nature into silent and static symbols void of being-ness and vitality," writes Enrique Salmón in *Eating the Landscape: American Indian Stories of Food, Identity, and Resilience*.[17] Videos and virtual-reality learning do not substitute for direct engagement. "Vitalism," as William Drury Jr. wrote in *Chance and Change-Ecology for Conservationists*, is more than a "mystical alternative to materialistic science."[18]

Students in our riparian garden engage with the plants using all their senses. They touch them, with permission; smell them, with their noses; view their intricate structures through a hand lens; and eat them after appropriate discussions about alkaloids and glycosides. Dedicated field instructors fill cracks in the mortar of their knowledge—"The fruits come after the flowers? I didn't know that"—that otherwise go undetected. Sites such as our riparian forest serve as ad hoc educational nature centers in the city, augmenting the small network of established places. Sensory memories embed deeply, strengthening their foundational core.

The semester had ended, and I was dusting the rolltop desk in Matt's office. I glanced at the pile of field notebooks that were waiting to be graded, and curiosity got the better of me. I leafed through one notebook and was delighted by the sketches the student had made of the plants they had met. On the margin, one had written, "I tasted a wild berry!" exclamation point included, the student clearly feeling proud. My mind flew to the Yaqui Deer Singers, about whom I had just been reading. There is a Yaqui community not far away, in the town of Guadalupe. The Deer Singers, by cultural tradition, sing of flowers and dance open the door to other worlds.

Maybe that dancing seed really *was* part of our group.

GLOBE CHAMOMILE: DANCING IN THE RAIN

It is two days past the summer solstice. The first big thunderclouds of the monsoon season are rumbling in. They have blown their way north across the expanse between Tucson and Ahwatukee and are climbing over the hills of South Mountain into Phoenix. *Here they come!* Matt and I and Mak, who squeezed in between, are on the blue loveseat on the porch watching the show. While we wait, we chat about our favorite clouds—the lenticular ones in particular—but mostly we watch the birds. He points out an ash-throated flycatcher who landed in the velvet mesquite and, as I turn to look, I spot four house finches, mouths agape, vying for a turn at the water drip. A movement to the right, in the flame acanthus patch, turns out to be a young-of-the-year verdin sipping nectar, moving upside down and sideways to extract the sugary juice. Two Costa's hummingbirds, siblings most likely, are zipping across the bird bath and occasionally alighting for a drink. The mourning doves are mating again, on a branch of mesquite: not even an approaching storm can sway them from their favorite pastime of making more of themselves. A curve-billed thrasher lets loose an alarm call, refocusing our attention on the coming storm.

The rumbles of thunder become louder, the sky darkens with gray clouds, and the winds increase in velocity. I leave the porch to take a walk but quickly return to grab my basket because I see the wind blowing pods off the mesquite trees onto the cushions of plants below. The rules for the upcoming milling tell us to "pick pods from the trees and not from the ground" to avoid eating aflatoxins from fungi, but these pods are freshly fallen and have alit on aloe, agave, and dead stems of globe chamomile (*Oncosiphon pilulifer*). I add a mental asterisk, in keeping with the spirit of the law, to accommodate picking newly fallen pods from the layer of vegetation covering the ground.

As I am bending this way and that, like a verdin, to avoid being poked by spines, the rising humidity and winds whip the smells of the plants into a heady elixir. The chemical blend from creosote, alkali goldenbush (*Isocoma acradenia*), lantana, and globe chamomile seep into my being and engulf me. They make me happy and invigorated and whole.

I quickly dash back to the porch, basket in hand, because the winds are now gusting at 30 mph. The dust is darkening the sky and the weather alerts are pinging our phones. Then . . . it fizzles. The first rain cells pass us by. Monsoon rains are famously patchy. We sit back on the loveseat and keep waiting.

The raindrops eventually arrive, and the temperature drops thirty degrees Fahrenheit, it is only four in the afternoon, but it feels much later. In the coolness of the porch air, I stretch into Warrior Pose, and this turns into a dance because the nervous energy from the storm needs an outlet. I find myself dancing to the rhythm of the rain—*please* keep a comin', *please* keep a comin'—and I stomp-dance all the way to the end of the Saltillo tiles and back. Mak joins in for a couple of "leg under and throughs," he is the danciest of the four, and he is energized by the rain and the smells, too.

Matt adjusts the spigots that are pouring water from the roof into rain barrels and buckets, and then carries the pod-filled baskets into the house so the fruit won't get wet and grow fungus, and we all start to relax. The unexpected sound of crunching overtakes that

6

BEING ETHNOBOTANICAL

DRINK UP!

ANNA APPLE: REMEMBER HER NAME

I HAVE YET to visit Chiapas, Mexico, but in my readings, I learned of an anthropologist who has been tracking the ability of Tzeltal Mayan children to name plants along a trail.[1] Their capacity to do so has remained high over recent decades, despite ongoing change in their society. I doubt the same could be said for the plugged-in children in cities of my homeland. Young children have tremendous capacity for learning about creatures, but increasingly are engaging with human artifacts indoors and becoming better at identifying Pokémon 'species' than organisms such as oak trees.[2] References to nature are decreasing in fiction books, song lyrics, and film storylines, say social scientists, with dire consequences for conservation of biodiversity and caretaking of the plants that sustain us.[3] Ethnobotanical knowledge is woefully low.

On the bright side, many of my friends and neighbors can recognize and name an apple tree! Apple trees (*Malus domestica*) now live far beyond their ancestral home of Kazakhstan, thanks to characters like Johnny Appleseed who spread their seeds widely. One of my favorite memories of far-flung apple trees is backpacking to an abandoned orchard deep in the Superstition Mountains of Arizona.

FIGURE 14 Basket of apples in the orchard. Photo by Julie Stromberg.

Once there, we bounced excitedly from tree to tree, increasingly anticipating the new and different taste offered by each. So many flavor sensations. So many races in one small place! The trees were old, the Reavis family had moved away long ago, but the local aquifer was keeping them alive and fruitful. I packed as many as would fit into the form-fitting backpacks I had sewn for my trio of trail dogs, but by the time we arrived back at the jeep most had been jostled to mush. Three cheers for accidental applesauce!?

It is lovely, now, to have only to hike across the driveway to reach the Anna and Dorsett apple trees in our own little orchard. Last year, to allow the youngest of the four to focus on her personal growth (*me* time!), we nipped off her young fruit. Now, her rosy blush tells us, it is time for her first picking. She is loaded with apples, all of

FIGURE 15 Apples ready to be pressed into cider. Photo by Matt Chew.

them unmushed. Her long limbs spring into the air after each trio of apples detach into my palm, all that will fit, as if relieved to no longer be bearing that heavy load. Too much can break a girl.

Picking fruit is fun. And not just because of the chance to interact with the trees but also because of the anticipation of pleasure to come—apple cider! The per-cup cost of our first cider yield, after splurging on a home-made cider press, was sky high and the source of much humor about sustainable farming. But who, really, can put a price on the taste of the first sip, fresh off the press? Environmental economists, that's who![4] What a difficult job they have.

That first sip is indescribably delicious, but I will try. Liquid gold. Magical tartness. You *become* the apple. You *feel* her essence. And I doubt you will forget her name.

POMELO: FALLING OFF A PEDESTAL

Sharing the orchard with the rose family are the pomegranates (*Punica granatum*), figs (*Ficus carica*), and the rues, of which pomelo (*Citrus maxima*) is one of my favorites. Taste-wise, she is like grapefruit (*Citrus* × *paradisi*), only sweeter and milder. Citrus fruit, technically, are hesperidia—large berries with leathery rinds. I like to peel her rind and eat her juicy carpels straight off the tree.

But what a lot of work it is, in dry regions, to grow trees with juicy carpels. How did my great-great-grandfather manage, plowing soils in the Great Plains after living a lifetime in Sweden? It takes a bushel of education and a peck of sweat to become a good ecological partner. Farming is hard.

Not long after we planted our orchard, Matt and I attended a workshop on citrus growing where we realized just how much we were doing wrong. "Nitrogen deficiency" said the instructor when we showed him leaf samples from one of our trees. "Micronutrient deficiency, perhaps Fe or Mg, or Zn," for another. I cringed, shrinking into myself with shame. I knew our trees were not as healthy as they could be, but I didn't think I had been neglecting them. THUMP. Off my pedestal, I fell. Understand, at this time, I was volunteering at an animal shelter that focused on the vulnerable and I was perched high on my care-taking pedestal. I would cringe, in empathy, when I learned of someone abandoning their animal, leaving them without food or water. "How could someone *do* that?" became our daily mantra. How indeed.

Neglect, etymologically, means "failure to pick up." It is a form of abuse where the perpetrator is responsible for caring for someone who is unable to care for themself but fails to do so. Here I am, a botanist, and I have been depriving the orchard trees of nutrients. Letting down my end of our partnership. No juicy carpels for me, that day.

PARTY TIME

AGAVE: AWAITING THE BIG BANG

"Did you see anything new?" I asked Matt one fine spring day after his morning walkabout. "Just the hooded oriole hanging upside down, getting a drink from the aloe flowers." How nice to be able to take such sightings for granted.

Aloes look a bit like agaves, whether one is hanging upside down or not. The two can be hard to distinguish for those new to the Southwest unless they have taken a trip to the Desert Botanical Garden, a lovely place to spend time in the Sonoran Desert spring. The garden, which is eighty years old, was the brainchild of a small group of female Phoenicians who were tired of seeing the desert succumb to development. They wanted to preserve the local bounty and beauty before it was too late. That was almost a century ago!

Today, the Desert Botanical Garden serves to preserve, protect, and educate. If you visit, a volunteer will be eagerly waiting to explain the differences and similarities between these two lovely plants. You will understand convergent evolution. Agaves evolved in the Americas, aloes in Africa; they are in different families, not genetically close, but they look alike, each with a radial whorl of succulent leaves from which will emerge a tall spike of flowers. That is where these perennials part ways. Aloe sends up a new flowering stalk each year, while each individual of a clonal patch of agave produces them only once and then dies.[5] They go out with a big bang.

Agave and aloe both have trotted the globe and are fitting in nicely in their new lands, an assimilation of sorts, with the requisite period of adjustment. The flowers of *Agave americana*, in Africa as in America, provide food for visiting bats.[6] In our garden, we see new-world orioles poking their beaks into *Aloe vera*'s tubular flowers to sip nectar, much as the old-world ones do in Africa.[7]

Agave and aloe both are remarkable chemists. In addition to making sweets for pollinators, *Aloe vera* produces chemicals in her leaves which benefit my face. My northern European skin is not a good fit for the semitropical region in which I live. My first skin cancer appeared when I was forty-eight, and it served as a rude reminder of impending mortality. I have had several removed since, including the dreaded melanoma which gave me pause and infused new meaning into the "live in the moment" maxim but lately my skin seems healthier despite my increasing age. My dermatologist concurs.

The reason? I credit the plants and the salves therefrom. A growth hormone from *Aloe vera's* tissues stimulates wound healing in mine, while oils from the seeds of jojoba (*Simmondsia chinensis*), harvested by a wild crafter in Tucson, keep my skin moist.[8] I'm not precisely sure what biochemical effect the *Cannabis* salve is having on my skin, but I really don't care because it makes me feel young and alive.

Agave has her own set of assets. There are many species of Agave in the American Southwest, and many land races, each adapted to their locale and influenced by the humans who wild-tended them.[9] Agave has been used not just for food and drink, but for "fiber, cordage, clothing, sandals, nets, blankets, lances, fire hearths, musical instruments, hedgerows (including boundary demarcation), soap, medicine, and ceremonial purposes," writes Wendy Hodgson.[10] That is quite a long list.

The sun has set on my days of indulging in tequila sunrises, with their richly colored grenadine, but a sip now and then with friends is invigorating. Mezcal, too, will wake up the taste buds. And I am hoping, one day, to harvest, roast, and eat the sugar- and starch-filled "heart" of an agave—the embryonic inflorescence—from our garden. The oldest are twenty years old and have yet to bloom. I wonder when it will happen. Plant scientists are still trying to identify the hormones that regulate the timing of this programmed death; this grand risking of all for the next generation.[11] I *hope* we get to witness it.

When it does? I hope we don't take it for granted.

AN OVERFLOW OF MELONS

"Pass the biscuits, please!" Oh, Grandma's table. What a lively place that was. My brother Eric, especially, ate up the camaraderie, free-flowing conversation, and, of course, the food and drink. Grandma knew how to put out a home-grown spread.

During family trips to Kansas City, Missouri, Eric and I split time between the paternal and maternal sides of our tribe. Two different worlds, two spheres of belonging. The paternal side—my aunt's house—was prim and proper and wealthy and powerful. There, you had to prove yourself. You had to show your worth. Love and laughter flowed more freely at Grandma's. There, you could be yourself, relax, and have fun (especially when Teddy-the-dog snuffled your fingers). I did not know Grandma's husband, my maternal grandfather, but knew from stories that he was an avid gardener. His prize was his irises, which he cross-bred. He had a green thumb.

My mother, too, was a wonderful cook who enjoyed preparing meals. Me? Not so much. With one exception. When confronted with bounty from the garden? Then I go to town. I mean, stay home and cook! A bushel full of Tohono O'odham I'itoi onions (*Allium cepa var. aggregatum*) or an overflow of watermelons (*Citrullus lanatus*); they present a challenge. How many ways *can* one prepare a dish from big red pepos? After sating ourselves on watermelon salad, watermelon gazpacho, and watermelonade, one cucurbatious summer, we finally carted the remaining fruits to the local zoo in the back of the truck. The elephants enjoyed an unexpected treat. Next year, when the onions decided to be prolific, there was much French onion soup! Peeling away each layer of the fleshy, modified leaves made me think of a child repeatedly asking "why," going deeper, until they receive the answer that satisfies. Layer peeling is a good metaphor for thinking. It allows us to dig deep and unearth root causes.

Mostly, I like eating local because it helps me belong to my region. Let's parse this notion of belonging for a moment. There are many ways to do it. You can belong to a system and be integral to its function. You can belong to a tribe, based on common genetics or shared interests. You can belong to someone and be their property. My hackles were raised the other day, when I heard a botanist say, about a plant called mullein (*Verbascum thapsus*), who grows in the higher elevation terrain: "These *thugs* provide no help to pollinators and are choking out *our* native species." After giggling a little, imaging mullein as a murderous creature dressed in a sarong, I cringed at this notion that the native species were *his*. That they *belonged* to him—were his property to protect or control as he saw fit. Woman once were considered the property of men. Dogs still are, yet increasingly are viewed as companions. I don't want him to possess the indigenous plants, too. The plant world is not under *your* thumb, no matter how green you think yours is. And, my goodness, a check of the literature quickly negates that statement about pollinators.[12]

Whew. Let's go back to Grandma's. Let's open the door to a less "judgy" zone, where creatures are not subjected to a rigorous and biased check of competence and provenance as a basis for belonging.

Ah, the joy of a good rant. Now, how about those biscuits?

7

THE RECYCLERS

FLIES TO THE RESCUE

NOPAL DE CASTILLA: RECYCLING THE PADS

Nopal de Castilla (*Opuntia ficus-indica*) is an impressive cactus with thick succulent pads. This tall creature was used as a source of food and dyes by the Nazca people in Peru some 2,000 years ago and has traveled the world since, feeding humans and cows.[1] In our garden, she worms her way up through the branches of mesquite to display her demure orange flowers. Sometimes, after one of the ferocious swirlings of wind that seem to be happening more often, a passel of her pads will tumble to the ground. Some will grow into new plants, via vegetative reproduction: cast off a pad, clone away! Most of the pads, though, recycle back to the earth, assisted by flies.

Ah, flies. Butterflies and bees have become popular with the pollinator-loving public, but flies? Not everyone likes them. Especially when they are trying to suck your blood (looking at you, mosquitos). But there are many types of flies. There are many families within the order *Diptera*. Don't let one bad mosquito spoil the bunch, as the saying goes. I have identified sixty-six kinds of dipterans in our garden, to date (please note, I'm not ready to take

FIGURE 16 Robber fly (*Efferia* sp.) with honeybee (*Apis mellifera*). Photo by Julie Stromberg.

the relationship that far, just yet. I'm fine being friends). They have impressed me with their diversity in form and function.

Some of the flies have gorgeous wings and adorable faces, with great big eyes. Others, like the Tachinids, look like they have been quarantining and are in need a shave. But they all have a function. Flies collectively have many important jobs in the ecosystem.[2] Bee flies (*Bombyliidae*) and flower flies (*Syrphidae*) rival bees as pollinators in many regions and add to the functional diversity.[3] Other flies function as predators: White-tailed robber flies (*Efferia albibarbis*) keep populations of honeybees in check, as do the larvae of large-tailed aphid-eaters (*Eupeodes volucris*) for, ahem, populations of aphids. Flies also play a role simply by being food for others—trophic support is what that is called. The collective biomass of flies is key to sustaining insectivorous songbirds like willow flycatchers, and even nectar-feeders like hummingbirds require protein from insects when raising their young.

As to decomposition? That critical process that frees nutrients from organic matter to feed the primary producers? In my trip to the big compost pile in the back of our property, just now, I observed *three* different species of flies whose larvae feed on dead cactus pads.

In addition to feeding directly on the tissue, some serve as facilitators by transporting spores of fungi and bacteria as they tunnel through dead plant tissue. Hurrah for decomposers!

Flies, I believe, need a public relations manager to improve their image in the eyes of the public. Mexican cactus fly (*Copestylum mexicanum*) might make a good campaign mascot, or spokes-fly, if you prefer. She has beauty—a gorgeous blue-black body and iridescent wings—as well as talent: her young, at no charge, are one of the creatures who hasten decomposition of the pads that topple from nopal.[4] What more could you ask for? Oh, maybe butterfly wings?

GRAYTHORN: LADIES (NOT) FIRST!

Graythorn. What a name. She sounds like a character in a Tolkien saga, one that you want to be on your side in the race between good and evil. This shrubby denizen of riparian forest understories and rocky hillsides, with the scientific name of *Ziziphus obtusifolia*, is one we purchased at a nursery and planted. Her flowers aren't showy but are visited by many wasps and flies. Of course, visitation is not the same as pollination; not all who land on a flower depart with a grain of pollen or deposit one on a stigma, but many do.

I, myself, did not reproduce but take surprising comfort in knowing that other wild creatures are doing so. Reproductive biology of plants is fascinating, and it captured the attention of Charles Darwin for decades.[5] Plants have schemed an amazing variety of ways to encourage shuffling of genes to keep pace in an everchanging world while retaining, in many cases, the fallback option of having sex with oneself. The solutions to this evolutionary challenge are nonunique, in mathematics-speak.

Graythorn is one who has mastered the art of playing with time. Protandry, we call what she does. The stamens take the stage first while the pistils patiently wait. Once the "boys" are done, the females offer up their receptive stigmas to receive pollen from someone else's

FIGURE 17 Graythorn (*Ziziphus obtusifolia*). Photo by Julie Stromberg.

flower. No self-pollination for her.[6] It is satisfyingly symmetric to see flower flies visiting these flowers which, by virtue of ample nectar but little pollen, are classified as fly flowers. The commutative property springs to mind, as does my first female math teacher, in fifth grade, who taught it to me.

As to graythorn's reproductive success? The fly visits are followed by small berries which give rise to seedlings and then saplings. She is not prolific, but our garden environment is functioning as a *source* for her, and not a *sink*, in the lingo of metapopulation dynamics. She is spreading her good deeds far and wide.

RED WIGGLERS: LIVING YOUR PASSION

We may have a large compost pile, and a high diversity of flies and other decomposition specialists, but if you want to meet someone who is taking recycling to the next level? Go visit the Arizona Worm Farm, another biophilic green space in our neighborhood. They are passionate about red wiggler worms (*Eisenia fetida*), black soldier flies (*Hermetia illucens*), and other creatures who can help them in their quest to transform mega-piles of urban food waste and manure into nutrient-rich fertilizer.[7] They have made their vision a reality.

The black soldier flies at the worm farm are quite docile. You can walk right up and take a selfie with one, should you desire. The larvae of these *Stratiomyidae* feed on organic matter and transform it into useful products for farmers and gardeners. But the Arizona Worm Farm isn't just a decomposer's paradise: they have a food forest and egg-laying chickens. They sell sugar cane plants, aka *Saccharum officinarum* (sweet!) and stevia, aka *Stevia rebaudiana* (sweeter!), some of which are now growing in our garden, as well as other useful and beautiful plants.

The cutest members of the worm farm family? That would be the pair of rat terriers who attended doggy camp to learn how to put a dent in the populations of valley pocket gophers (*Thomomys bottae*), mice, and other small mammals who feed on the crops. Ha, the names of these wiggly little dogs! Matt and I have looked to the plant ~~Kingdom~~ Queendom over the years for the names of some in our own pack—Alfalfa, Macintosh, and Zookini—and added in the key component of photosynthesis when we adopted Sunshine. But those rat terriers take the cake. Teri and Guy are their nicknames, short for . . . bacteria and fungi. Way to pay homage to your passion. The sweetest yet!

YOU *CAN* FIGHT CITY HALL

TOWERING EUCALYPTS: TOLERANCE FOR SENESCENCE

"But," I protested, "this is a community landmark! They have cultural and biological significance. People stop along the street to chat about this pair of dead trees who tower above the rest. They ask about the hawks who nest in them or reminisce about the neighborhood. They are a touch stone, if you like. Please don't make us chop them down."

This was two decades ago, shortly after we moved in. After the irrigation had run dry and the trees had died. City inspectors, it seems, have low tolerance for senescence. The dead wood on our land was declared a fire hazard and an eye sore. We agreed, begrudgingly, to cart away most of the dead citrus trees if it meant the dead eucalypts could stay.

Red-tailed hawks, peregrine falcons, American kestrels, turkey vultures, phainopeplas, Gila woodpeckers, gilded flickers, western kingbirds, starlings, and even an osprey and great blue heron are among those we have seen nesting, mating, hunting, sleeping, or perching in these dead trees. The birds are "repurposing" the dead trees, which are called snags in the parlance of wildlife biologists.

The pair of trees are majestic, even if all that is left is the skeleton. The skin is long gone—the thin outer layer of phloem and bark. The leaves, of course, are no more, having been transformed into mulch. The skeletal remains themselves are not bone—not mineral, like ours—but are wood. Lignified xylem. The xylem tissue no longer conducts water but persists as heartwood, providing structural support. They continue to stand tall.

The longitudinal array of xylem cells—the grain of the wood—is distinctive in each genus of tree. I spent hours during my career peering at vascular tissue under the microscope, measuring annual rings and appreciating the subtle differences in cell size and shape. Seasoned woodworkers can tell the identity of a tree by looking at

FIGURE 18 Turkey vulture perching in eucalyptus snag. Photo by Matt Chew.

the patterns. They know, too, to cut *with* the grain. Cutting against it carries risks. And sometimes rewards.

Within the bird world, Gila woodpeckers and gilded flickers are the woodworkers. They use their strong, sharp beaks to chisel holes in the trees in which they, and other cavity-nesting birds, will nest.[8] The cavities buffer the babies against the weather. The anatomy and physiology of the woodpeckers buffer them from the shock of the pounding.[9] "Pounding your head against the wall" is a phrase with which you may be familiar and one which goes hand in hand with "you can't fight city hall." Performing an act over and over without achieving resolution is an exercise in frustration. Sometimes, though? We get lucky. In some cities around the world, the value of dead trees for wildlife is being recognized. In Canberra, Australia, the ancestral home of the eucalypts, some snags have been dubbed totem trees and are protected.[10] They are pruned for public safety but left to stand.

The city inspector who visited our house, those decades ago, was a woman. I like to think the notion of community and culture spoke to her heart. She seemed to soften in response to my plea to let our sentinels stand. I am grateful to this day for her decision to go against the city grain. Her act took bravery. And a tinge of wildness.

Hmm. Rather than trying to *fight* city hall? Maybe we try to educate. And speak from the heart.

MORE DEAD THINGS: THE BEE TREE

Another inhabitant of the eucalypt snags is the valley carpenter bee. They are aptly named. These very large bees, the females black and the males yellow, are the woodpeckers of the bee world, boring holes with their mandibles to make homes for *their* babies. Tiny holes, by comparison. Almost one centimeter in diameter. They go to trade school to learn their skill so they can come home and build homes for their community. Or something like that. If we want to be scientific about it, and we probably should, it *is* true that bees learn.[11] Eusocial bees (like honeybees) seem more adept at learning than do solitary bees, entomologists say, or at least have been more thoroughly studied. Bees learn better when allowed to explore on their own, rather than following a set rubric, a message with relevance to the educational approach for *our* children. Some bees are geniuses, making more innovative or efficient choices than the rest!

Valley carpenter bees fall somewhere in the middle on the spectrum of sociality, forming small communities of sisters, children, and sometimes unrelated females. They are faring well in forested cities. *Someone* is doing a good job at home-schooling. Wood-nesters, in general, fare better in cities than the ground-nesting bees given all the mowing and trampling that occurs. Special care is needed to set aside protected ground for the soil-nesters, in city parks and private gardens, accompanied by little signs to explain.

FIGURE 19 Nests of solitary bees in dead Mexican palo verde (*Parkinsonia aculeata*). Photo by Julie Stromberg.

There is one other special dead tree in our garden. In a burst of creativity, we named her the "Bee Tree." The dead body of this Mexican palo verde is full of small holes created by cactus woodborer bees (*Lithurgopsis*), close relatives of the leafcutters (*Megachile*). After chewing a tunnel in the tree with her mandibles, a mother woodborer bee will provision her nest with a ball of pollen she collected from the western prickly pear cactus (*Opuntia engelmannii*) nearby. Then she will lay an egg and seal the exposed end. She had better be vigilant, though, because a mother kleptoparasitic cuckoo wasp (*Chrysura*) may be nearby, waiting her chance to dart in and replace the egg with her own. That wasp doesn't have the skills to make or provision her own home, but she is very pretty. And very, very quick.

Other trees who continue to give after death, and who leave a nice inheritance, are the fan palms (*Washingtonia filifera* and hybrids). The other day, I was rearranging the outdoor furniture—and by furniture, I mean the sections of dead palm trunk we repurposed into outdoor seating—and inadvertently caused the Great Disruption of 2022. To a population of yellow carpenter ants (*Camponotus fragilis*) anyway. These big and beautiful southwestern endemics seemed friendly but confused. I hope they managed to rebuild. They are nicer neighbors than the red harvester ants (*Pogonomyrmex barbatus*), if we are going to name names. The presence of those big red stingy creatures requires one to wear long pants and sneakers while gardening, even though shorts and sandals would be cooler, but they mostly leave us alone because we have learned to mostly leave them alone.

So, to recap. For observing carpenter bees, woodborer bees, and carpenter ants? Any attire is appropriate. For harvester ants, carpenter pants are required. You know, those sturdy pants with lots of pockets. I apologize for that bit of silliness, but I'm a *plant* biologist. My attention span for the six-legged sometimes is not great. The plants always lurk, ready to *snag* my attention.

CLOSING ECOLOGICAL LOOPS

OUR FUNGAL FRIENDS

Oooh, I love the smell of fresh soil. I love playing in the dirt. Maybe I'm part beagle. The odors released from the soil-dwelling fungi call to me. Of course, fungi do more than amuse our noses: "Fungi are powerful players in global bio-geochemistry, recycling carbon and mobilizing nitrogen, phosphorus and other bioelements," say researchers.[12] They influence who germinates in the soil[13] and support the growing plants by living inside their bodies. In river bottoms, and in arid uplands too, velvet mesquite is one of the trees who collaborates with a kind of fungi called arbuscular mycorrhizae.[14] These fungi who live inside her roots extend their threadlike bodies into the crevices of the soil, increasing the flow of nutrients to *her* body. Carbohydrates flow to the fungi in exchange. Also perhaps flowing through the bodies of the mycorrhizal fungi? Communication signals. Chemicals may be flowing from one tree to another, warning neighbors of the presence of herbivores. Or, if resources become scarce, an older tree might share food with a sapling by means of her fungal friend. "Inter-plant communication through mycorrhizal networks mediates complex adaptive behaviour in plant communities," says one team of researchers.[15] I hope this is happening in our garden. I hope such intimate partnerships are reforming in our long-used Rillito soils.

Those who study the fungi, the mycologists, do powerful work. I first fell in love with fungi when I explored the forests of Wisconsin. I loved learning about stinkhorns, dead man's fingers, and deadly amanitas (who needs Halloween when you have the North Woods?). I almost became a mycologist myself.

The world could use more of them. Astoundingly, less than 10 percent of the estimated total species of fungi, worldwide, a whoppingly low number, have been described and named. "The taxonomy of this group has a turbulent history that is only now starting to be settled with the advent of genomics and phylogenomics," say experts in the field.[16] The fungal world is far removed for our own, having diverged from our branch of the tree of life a very long time ago. Many are not inclined to reproduce sexually, or do so subsurface, and are only identified as morphs. If it was not clear, I was referring in that last sentence to fungi and not to those who study them. The tally of fungal species in our garden is woefully low. Desert shaggy mane (*Podaxis pistillaris*), common fieldcap (*Agrocybe pediades*), and witch's butter (*Tremella mesenterica*) are a few that occur, as well as dog's vomit fungus (*Fuligo septica*) (ew!) which is not a fungus at all but a slime mold within Queendom Protista. The fungi on my list are the ones who parade their colorful and stalked spore-releasing parts above ground. Members of the *Glomus* genus and some other mycorrhizal symbionts aren't as flamboyant. They produce their spores underground, at the tips of their hyphal bodies. One needs a microscope to detect them.

A long history of agricultural use, especially if heavy equipment and toxic chemicals are involved, can deplete a soil of its fungal lifeforms or alter their composition. As time passes after a farm field is abandoned, the fungi can shift from fast-growing taxa to slower growing ones, similar to patterns in the plant community, and decomposition can shift from predominantly bacterial in nature to predominantly fungal.[17] I wish a knowledgeable mycologist would survey our soil and roots. I want to know if we should inoculate mesquite with mycorrhizal fungi to improve soil fertility as is done in degraded soils around the world, or if those fungal collaborators already here.[18] I want to know who is making those lovely smells the earth is releasing to my nose.

When I'm through sniffing and ready to depart this earth? Please dig a hole and bury me in the ground, as is. No embalming fluids, no wooden box. Just wrap me in a thin cotton blanket, toss me in, and let the fungi feast.

HAY IS FOR HORSES

"Hay," nickered the horse. "Hey, yourself," I bantered back. "Give me some *hay*, lady!" I wish I could talk to horses. I am not horse-savvy like some of my friends. I see the neighbor's horses nearly every day, and Chip and Mak bark at them, trying to engage them in play, but they remain a mystery to me.

I know they are American paint horses (*Equus ferus caballus*), and I know that our neighbors breed them and sell them. Several years back, they and other small-scale breeders weathered a slump in the market. Or would that be a swayback in the market. I don't know. "Pee ranches" had sprung up, stabling pregnant mares in tight stalls, to collect hormone-filled urine.[19] The hormones were extracted by pharmaceutical companies and marketed to aging women whose internal supply was diminishing. The foals were sold, which flooded the market, and the cycle repeated anew. The pregnant mare urine (PMU) farms, as they also were called, were eventually outlawed in the United States, and soya beans (*Glycine max*) and yams (*Dioscorea* sp.) stepped up as alternative sources of hormones. Plants to the rescue! Our neighbors remained solvent.

The only bodily waste we have personally benefited from, with respect to horses, is manure. Horse manure is drier and less odorous than cow manure, and we occasionally receive a load or two from the neighbors. Dung, be it from horses or rabbits, sustains an amazing diversity of coprophilous fungal life.[20] In some parts of the world, horse dung sustains powerful members of the *Psilocybe* genus who not only transform complex organic compounds into simpler ones but transform one's perception of the life around them. In a good, mind-expanding way. The horse manure needs to age for a while, like a fine wine, as the decomposers do their job but soon becomes food for the trees in the orchard.

Thankfully, more partnerships are arising between livestock farms and plant farms, closing an ecological loop. Some still view manure as a waste product and ship it to landfills, but others are learning the benefits of respecting ecological cycles.[21]

"Hey, where are you going with that truckload? Bring it over here, please!"

TERMITES: MAGICAL MOMENTS

The sky is ablaze with flight! Western pipistrelle bats (*Parastrellus hesperus*), lesser nighthawks, dragonflies—the swooping and darting of these aerial predators is spectacular. Where did they all come from? We don't know! Why are they here? For the dinner party! Someone must have sent an invitation. The first big rain of the summer has fallen. A full inch in yesterday's thunderstorms. We wait in anticipation for the first big rain as, I imagine, do they. The part of me that likes to watch wild creatures feast is jumping up and down with joy.

What is on the menu? Winged termites! Not the western drywood termites (*Marginitermes hubbardi*) who feed on the wood of our house, for which we call the termite-control man. And not the fungus-farming termites of the deserts of Africa, who weed out certain fungi so as to encourage the ones who can digest the intractable lignins that give plants their sturdy cell walls. No, these are desert encrusting termites (*Gnathamitermes* sp.), who need a more endearing name. But they do indeed encrust dead herbaceous plants and twigs with saliva-filled mud and then eat the dead matter for dinner, leaving hollowed-out tubes on the ground.[22]

Right now, at dusk, the reproductive caste of these eusocial termites is soaring high into the air to mate. The desert comes alive after rain! Winged particles of food are soaring into the air! Those who evade the predators will make more or themselves. More termites mean more recycling, less accumulation of dead plant matter, and lower risk of wildfire. The actions of the termites also increase infiltration of water, which helps the plants grow. Detritivores to the rescue!

Twenty years in, if the city inspector should stop by again? I think she would be pleased by what she sees. She may even want to put the termites on the payroll of the Public Works Department, but there is no need. Their ecosystem services are free.

8

THE ECOTHERAPISTS

AROMATHERAPY

ELEPHANT TREE: KEEPING US CALM

S HE'S NOT so much a tree as a tall shrub. But she packs a powerful punch, to use a violent analogy for the potency of her ability to calm.

"Get up, sleepy head, there is a surprise for you!" It is Sunday morning, and I am luxuriating in the last few moments of sleep. Waking up slowly is lovely: no alarm clock, no rush, just dancing in and out of the last delicious moments of one's dream.

We had purchased her at a nursery. During visits to the small desert mountain range we see from our windows, we fell in love with this shrub in the torchwood family and, especially, with her redolent odors.[1] She, like her relatives from the Arabian Peninsula, frankincense tree (*Boswellia* spp.) and African myrrh (*Commiphora africana*), makes a deep impression on the human nose.[2]

The surprise was that elephant tree (*Bursera microphylla*) was blooming. Her tiny flowers, with their ring-shaped nectaries, were attracting dozens of tiny flies and tiny bees. But her powerful smells come not so much from these ephemeral bits as from her more permanent parts. The more we brushed her leaves, as we leaned in to focus, the more frequent were the wafts of resin-filled air. It smelled like heaven.

I suppose it was fitting that it was Sunday. In some churches around the world, aromatic resins of torchwood are placed in thuribles and burned as ceremonial incense to help transport worshippers to a place of peace. Ethnobotanical studies confirm that her volatile resinous compounds, which serve to protect her body, reduce the anxiety in ours. To that, I say, "amen."

Keep the surprises coming.

MOUNTAIN LAUREL: STAYING IN SNIFF-SHAPE

Crinkle. Crinkle. Crinkle. What the heck? I jumped out of bed, nine years back, to the sound of paper ripping. Amusingly enough, I found our curious new pup having a micro-adventure. Chip had come to us from the streets of Phoenix with a gash on his lovely brown head. I worked like the dickens to keep him socialized and open to the new. It worked. Now, the mischievous boy had removed a book auspiciously titled *Inside of a Dog: What Dogs See, Smell and Know* from a shelf and was noisily proceeding to eat it.[3] Parts of the book were now, literally, inside of a very specific dog. Reading the uneaten parts of the book was a fun adventure for me, providing the opportunity to explore the world from the viewpoint of another species. I love to play that game.

I do, sometimes, put nose to the wind, to determine if I can tell what is engaging our pack of four. Sometimes, I can; more often, not. Sense of smell decreases with age, and I now find myself test-sniffing the strong scents, and the weak, to make sure I've still "got it," "it" being the capacity to engage with my environment though my nose. Females on *average* have greater olfactory sensitivity than males, detecting scents at lower concentrations, and have greater capacity to discriminate and name them, once sensed.[4] But, alas, mine is fading. To slow the decline, I exercise my sense of smell frequently. Use it or lose it, as they say.

Thankfully, even within the confines of our garden, there are many opportunities to keep in sniff-shape. In February, the bright scents of orange blossoms (*Citrus sinensis*) elevate our serotonins *and* our mood. In April, the bees and I swoon, if I dare use that word, to the earthy aroma of catclaw acacia (*Senegalia greggii*). On May mornings, like the honeybees who bask in the narcotic nectar of her trumpet-shaped flowers, I lose myself in the soul-enchanting smells of sacred datura (*Datura wrightii*).

I skipped over March in that sequence, which is a good time of the year to skip with delight. This is when the glorious blossoms of Texas mountain laurel (*Dermatophyllum secundiflorum*) appear. These riparian denizens of the Chihuahuan ecoregion have been planted in many an urban landscape, including our own. Almost better than the purple color of her flowers is her smell. Grape candy, grape Kool-Aid ... the odor is intense and magnificent. She attracts valley carpenter bees, migrating flutters of painted ladies (*Vanessa cardui*), and us. Sometimes I can be found atop my stepladder, enjoying a front row seat to the show.

Ah, the smells of spring. Plants are spectacular chemists, producing compounds like limonene and linalool—and verbenene and sabinol.[5] Those would be good names for our next group of dogs! Whether produced in leaf glands or along nectar trails, whether repelling insects or attracting them, we receive ancillary benefit. Fancifully enough, these chemicals have no odor, per se. Through trial and error, over the millennia, our brains and sensory apparatus developed the ability to discriminate among chemical compounds and attach a scent-memory to each in our neural network. Qualia. Experiencing properties as distinct from their physical source; a tipping point between physical and metaphysical. Almost enough to tip me off my ladder.

CATCLAW ACACIA: THE JOY OF BIRD SONG

Catclaw acacia is one of those small-leaved legume trees who grows along ephemeral streams in the American Southwest. She is xero-riparian. Another of her common names is wait-a-minute bush and she will not hesitate to snag you with her recurved claws if you approach too close. But I overlook this trait. Swooning can do that to a girl.

Catclaw's gifts don't stop at perfume. Her spiny branches provide secure spots for bird nests, which might otherwise blow down in the gusts of wind we often receive in lieu of rain. Her limbs in our garden are dotted with nests of verdins, a small passerine bird. Verdins wisely make more than one nest per year, perhaps to confuse the snakes who would eat their eggs but also to adjust to the changing weather. Unlike many birds, they live in nests all year long and build them to different specifications depending on season. Summer nests have thinner walls than winter ones; spring-nests are oriented away from the prevailing winds and summer nests with them.[6] They have desert living down to a fine art.

Matt and I love our bird-filled garden. "We are not *just* listers," he reminds. Yes, we get excited by the migrants and never-before-seens, but we also revel in the everyday birds—the year-round residents who have become part of our extended family, and what they *do*. I love watching Abert's towhees dance their two-steps, searching for bugs in the ground. It is thrilling to be surprised by a brazen greater roadrunner strutting across the porch rafters, chasing lizards. Being inside a flock of lesser nighthawks, at dusk, as they swoop past our heads to catch dinner, can brighten my darkening mood.

Their songs are perhaps what I like best about them, as I am not adept at visual birding. The females of many bird species are as vocal as the males in some regions, if not more, which we know because female scientists are becoming more vocal themselves and are drawn to investigate those of their own sex.[7] "Historically, bird song has been regarded as a sex-specific signaling trait; males sing to attract females and females drive the evolution of signal exaggeration by preferring males with ever more complex songs" says a scientist named Katharina; "However, we now know that female song is common."[8]

My relationship with bird song is a bit playful. When I hear someone asking, "Who cooks for you?" I know the white-winged doves are about. A demanding cry for "cream of wheat!" denotes a curve-billed thrasher. Northern cardinals have many songs and calls to keep in contact, impress a mate, defend territory, warn of threats, and pay me a mood-boosting compliment: "Pretty, pretty, pretty!" they proclaim. The acrobatic verdin, hanging upside down in catclaw, frequently casts an accusation, "*She* did it!"

The healing power of bird song is becoming well known.[9] The effects of their judgements? The jury is still out.

FRACTALICIOUS

PECAN TREES: BECKONING LIMBS

Ninety-year-old pecan trees (*Carya illinoinensis*). A whole grove. Let me into those beckoning limbs!

The Farm at South Mountain, several miles to the east, is a restful place to eat locally grown, pesticide-free food. The picnic tables under

FIGURE 20 Pecan tree (*Carya illinoinensis*) at the Farm at South Mountain. Photo by Julie Stromberg.

the grove of pecans are a sanctuary for meeting with friends during pandemics. I am grateful to those who have nurtured this green space and protected it from the tidal wave of urban development.

While my lunch companion was fetching our food (hmm, what am I in the mood for . . . pecan salad or egg sandwich?), I was mentally calculating the route I would take up the tree if allowed. Then I found myself enthusing about forest bathing to a stranger who had come over to chat, perhaps having noticed an odd gleam in my eye. The practice, I explained, which is called *shinrin-yoku* in Japan, has gained traction in parts of the world.[10]

Trees do so much for us! They provide the oxygen we breathe and the food we eat (*thank you*). They bolster our immune system and lengthen our lives. Their fractal-filled canopies and odor-filled flowers and bark cause our brain waves to slow, our blood pressure to drop, and our body to relax.[11] Which ultimately makes us more productive. This is not magical thinking, I assured her: it is supported by respected researchers at revered institutions.

And it is not just the trees who help us. The composition and diversity of *all* the plants makes a difference. Blue flowers make us calmer than red ones. Complex landscapes make us more creative. Women are particularly affected: when we are deprived of access to nature, we become more stressed than the men.[12] If you want to learn more, I gushed, check out the book *The Nature Fix* by Florence Williams![13]

"Ah, you are back! Let's tuck in. Yum, these pecans are delicious." The food at the Farm fills our bodies. The wooded setting feeds our souls. Okay, *that* may be magical thinking. And the isolation of the pandemic makes some of us atypically chatty.

"Oh, be sure to look up *fractals* and become amazed by the similarity between the patterns the tree branches make and the patterns our retinas use when scanning the landscape, I didn't have time to explain," I prattled to the baffled stranger on the way out, after my companion and I had finished our meal.

Hmm. Perhaps I should have gone up that tree after all. Not everyone is in the mood for a lecture.

CHASTE TREE: SPIKES OF BLUE

Colors are part of a language which preceded words. Yellow, red, green; each hue makes us feel something different and each means something different to those who are paying attention. Red arouses us and alerts us to ripe or poisonous fruit, yellow excites us, and the shorter wavelengths of the greens and blues make us calm. These facts are not lost on the marketers.[14]

In my teenage years, during the long dark Wisconsin winter, I recall playing a personality-reveal game based on cards of different color. As the daylength became ever shorter, my color preferences shifted, trending to gray and black. Yipes! Mental health alert. Blue, these days, is my favorite color. The blue of the cloudless sky is magnificent and seemingly boundless, but rare in the biotic world. Blue is a challenging hue for organisms to produce.

Chaste tree (*Vitex agnus-castus*) is one of the blue-flowered beauties in our garden. This small Mediterranean tree was a volunteer, having spread from yards where she was planted. Her name evokes queries. Does she really lower your libido, or that of your mate, if you drink her tea? You could try some and see!

Another blue beauty who happens to grow in our garden is guayacán (*Guaiacum coulteri*). And by *happens*, I mean we made our annual pilgrimage to the Desert Botanical Garden plant sale and paid out a goodly chunk of money. Worth it! One of guayacán's relatives is the source of the bioactive agent in the cough-medicine marketed as Mucinex. I don't know about you, but I find that I trust a medicine more if the label is blue I am familiar with the plant who produced it.

Some plants make their blues by de-acidifying a group of pigments called anthocyanins, which typically flash red. So clever! Others do so by chelating, or bonding, these same pigments with magnesium.[15] Magnesium, you may recall from Introductory Botany, is a silvery-white alkaline earth metal and one that plants already use at the center of their chlorophyll molecules. So innovative!

Perhaps the most thrilling aspect of guayacán and chaste tree, beyond their medicinal teas and piercing blues? The awareness that the chlorophyll they make, with magnesium, is chemically similar to the hemoglobin we make, with iron, to internally transport the oxygen they give us.

We are not so different after all. Thinking about that makes me radiate bright yellow vibes.

SWEETBUSH: CHASING THE BLUES AWAY

"Where is Chase?" I asked Matt, with a tinge of worry. "I can't find him anywhere." I tromped around the inner yard and, eventually, in a hidden corner, found the big guy cowering behind a yellow-flowered bush—a sweetbush, in case you were wondering. Unmoving. Frozen in his world. "What's wrong, big fellow?" "Come here," I cooed. He would not budge.

This was a year before our most recent rescue, Suzie, arrived. We were fostering a shelter dog who had the blues. His mental state was apathetic, pessimistic, and unmotivated. Anhedonic. Chase's home life had changed. He had been relegated to the backyard, for weeks, ignored and neglected, after his human became ill. Day after long day passed. He would *bark* to go in, and the door did not open. He *scratched* at the wood, and nothing changed.

Depression emanates from our cognitive brain—thinking-gone-awry—as much as from our emotion-based limbic system. If we are in settings where we learn helplessness and hopelessness, our mammalian brains begin to extrapolate failure and inadequacy from the specific to the general. We spiral downward. Finally, a concerned relative made a phone call, and Chase found his way to the shelter. There, in the play yard, he hid. In his kennel, he stayed in the back, head held low. Eyes blank. And chased his tail. Repeatedly. Hence, his name. He was looking for safe connection with another but finding none. He was deteriorating.

I leapt at the chance to foster him when the shelter staff asked, hoping that life in our quiet, multidog home would transform him—which it did! But, oh, what a challenge. He didn't know *what* to do, at first, except chase his tail. Matt gave generously of

FIGURE 21 Sweetbush (*Bebbia juncea*). Photo by Julie Stromberg.

his time, and Chase responded. Yet, it was slow, unsteady progress. Chase, safe in his bed, watched as we went about our daily rituals. He watched our pack getting kisses and being dressed for walks (collars *on!*). He heard our conversations and games, and he smelled our happiness and treats. Part of him *so* wanted to be part of that. He plodded his big, brindle self into the living room, took a quick peek, and then turned and plodded back out, to engage with his tail.

What to do? During my undergraduate days, in a chemistry lecture, the concept of activation energy grabbed my attention. To initiate a chemical reaction, one must sometimes input a bit of energy. To bring about a change, one must sometimes give a nudge. Perhaps it was the elevating odors from sweetbush. I'm not sure. But there in the corner, with Chase, we had a transformative moment. Out of somewhere, a force of positive energy billowed up, propelling the words "Let's go Chase, let's run," and up he came, and we ran around the yard. A spark of adrenaline. He came *alive*.

After that, Chase began to follow us on our walkabouts, our loops around our garden. He began sniffing the scent-laden trails and perking his ears at the bird song. He became softly fascinated by the lizards scampering at his feet and the butterflies fluttering above; stimulated but not overly so. An intermediate disturbance, of sorts. Ecotherapy was working its magic. His brain was learning, once again, to encode positive memories. More and more, that tail, he ignored it.

Soon, restorative sleeps under his collar and beneficial neurotransmitters replenished, he began to venture *outside* the gate. One day, on a slow walk down the path, we stopped under the Indian rosewood tree (*Dalbergia sissoo*) to say "hello" to a horse who lived there. The two of them snuffled muzzles. Then he *smiled*. Chase looked from the horse, to me, and slowly smiled. Finally, *there* is your personality. Ebullient and effusive are not words anyone will tag you with, but calm, gentle, and quietly hopeful; those will do.

Finally, that lovely day arrived, the one that foster parents await. "Chase has been adopted," the matchmakers called to say. He had found a new home. Thank you, garden, for helping heal this boy.

Special shout-out to you, sweetbush, for chasing the blues away.

HEALING THE PLANTS

SACRED DATURA: PLANTS GET SICK, TOO

Oh my gosh that made me laugh! I was chatting with a couple at the animal shelter who were hoping to adopt a dog, one who had finally turned the corner and been nursed back to health after a long illness. "What is the name of that virus?" the taller of the pair asked, trying to remember. "It begins with a 'd' . . . dystopia?" I tried hard to swallow my chuckle. He was close. Distemper is what he was aiming for. If only! If only dystopia, too, could be prevented by vaccine.

Not that viruses are inherently amusing. Of course, they aren't. I have had my own share of down time from one virus or another, following stress and overwork. Not fun. It is fun, though, to think about viruses. They are the most abundant life form on the planet, it seems.[16] Only some are active at any one time, in an ecosystem, with the rest being inactive but forming "a potential population for recruitment, much like a seed-bank in plant populations" say

FIGURE 22 Sacred datura (*Datura wrightii*). Photo by Julie Stromberg.

researchers.[17] They are a busy lot, exchanging strings of nucleotides, crossing species boundaries, and developing into new types.

So far, in our tally of taxa in the garden, only two plant viruses have made the list, and their identity remains uncertain. Identifying viruses requires a well-equipped lab, and we have enough dogs. Pardon another lame joke but we do, seriously, have enough dogs. Only one is part labrador.

Thinking about viruses takes one into interesting eddies. It swirls our brains around the boundaries between living/nonliving and self/non-self. Some 8 percent of our own genome is viral DNA, studies show, revealing a deep legacy of past interactions.[18] Some virologists are challenging the dogma, asking novel questions, and finding that some viruses, can, in fact, be beneficial. Viruses shuttle genes between organisms and don't always cause disease. Some virologists are seeking, and finding, cases of mutualism and symbiosis with viral partners.

Still, it's hard not to think *pathogen* when one thinks *virus*. Sadly, I just discovered that one of the most sanctified inhabitants of our garden has fallen ill. Sacred datura. She is an herbaceous perennial, with stems that die back at summer's end and reemerge in spring from meristems, those growing tips more commonly called buds. She has a deep history with humans: shamans and Western doctors alike have been drawn to her powerful (and dangerous) chemicals—her nitrogen-rich tropane alkaloids—to engage in spiritual flights or treat diseases like Parkinson's.[19] The bees who are drawn to her scent emerge in a stupor after drinking her nectar; I have helped more than one climb out of her blossoms. I, myself, have taken a calming bath in her leaves, and perhaps will do so again. And now *she* is sick!

Plants, good multicellular creatures that they are, have immune systems to defend against pathogens, be they bacteria, fungi, nematodes, oomycetes (the damping-off fungi which turn out to not be fungi after all), or viruses.[20] Their immune systems differ from ours in various ways, of course, but they get the job done. Mostly. Like us, when under acute or chronic stress, when malnourished, or when near a concentration of vectors, some of them succumb.

Poor datura! Her leaves are curling inward like an arthritic hand and are blotched with yellow. I'm not certain of the name of the virus. Plant doctors aren't as common as animal doctors, for consultation. Tomato chlorosis virus? Tomato yellow leaf curl virus? Or, ye God, both? Sacred datura is in the tomato family, and we planted tomato (*Solanum lycopersicon*) in our porch bed. Did we put her at risk, by bringing in an infected one? Is this where the fear of "other" arose, long ago? "[A]n ever-increasing portion of Earth's natural landscapes lie adjacent to agricultural lands" say researchers, and these "agro-ecological interfaces are surprisingly porous and biologically interactive."[21]

I don't know what I can do to help her. Some plant scientists are experimentally infusing plants with compounds that may augment their own capacity to defend, and others are exploring the role of mycorrhizal fungi in protecting plants from disease. Hurry up, scientists: submit those grants! And while you are at it, can you work on that vaccine for dystopia?

FIG TREES: HEALING, NOT HEELING

I have not traveled to the Indian subcontinent, but I visit a tiny piece of it each time I go to the animal shelter. A large fig tree (*Ficus* sp.) casts her dense shade over the Snuffle Garden. She is out of her wet tropical habitat, but the dogs and dog walkers appreciate her large evergreen leaves, as do the great-tailed grackles.

Volunteers walk the shelter trails with the dogs not just to exercise their limbs, but to help them heal. No, not heel, heal. But the shelter garden itself, when I first began volunteering, needed love. Caretaking of urban landscapes has become a noisy exercise in demonstrating that one has the money to hire "guns" to clip plants into submission. Control is taken as evidence of care. Many abuses can be normalized.

I made waves at the shelter, a few years back, a small tsunami even, when I could no longer bear the wholescale application of orange-tinted herbicide to suppress growth of grasses under the irrigated trees: imagine a gallery with Monets on the wall and toxic chemicals on the floor. I could not tolerate the harsh pruning of creosote bushes into cubes: imagine a sculpture of Aphrodite, the Greek goddess of love and beauty, with her arms cut off. Imagine a pit bull puppy, with ears cut off by scissors. Yes, I went there. There are appropriate ways to prune.[22] Effective urban gardening demands skilled and respectful workers with commensurate pay.

My proposal for a trial period of a poison-free but fractal-filled section of trail, to be monitored and compared to a control, was well received. To hasten the regrowth, I transferred seeds from our garden—annual sunflower, desert marigold (*Baileya multiradiata*), parry penstemon (*Penstemon parryi*), and others—to this new garden, where they are filling the trails with beauty and filling the insects and birds with food. And when springtime came? After the winter rains? A suite of desert annuals, who had persisted in the soil in seed form for who knows how long, emerged to set seed themselves, freed, finally, from the onslaught of herbicide. The plants, dogs, and dog walkers all seem happier. The grackles do, too.

Snuffle away, pups, snuffle away.

9

GETTING PHYSICAL

CLIMBING INTO THE CANOPY

MY LEGS

I LOVE MY legs. They may be short, but they are strong. They hang me upside down in trees and push shovel into ground to plant one. They run me across hills, accommodating bump and dale. When I run in the mountains, the small range I see from my south window, my legs merge with the granite. Powerful. Solid. Those mountains are permanent. From the waist up, I am "me," thinking, watching, breathing . . . but those legs of mine, they have a mind of their own. Half mountain, half me. They fly across the trail. They are free.

Runner's high is real! Over the millennia, our bodies developed systems that rewarded us for physical endurance and kept us long-loping for hours. Pain-suppressing endorphins, like those found in opium poppy (*Papaver somniferum*), are released well into the run. Another group of chemicals, including anandamide—a cannabinoid similar to those produced by *Cannabis sativa*—are released earlier, giving us a more immediate thrill on the hill.[1]

Early in my academic career, on weekends, to give my body some playtime, I would run mile after mile on desert trails. While my brain was chewing on some analytical morsel or practicing a talk for a conference, my body would *become* a panther, fast-pacing the perimeter of my territory. (I run more slowly, now. More of a shuffle, really.) On a lark, one day, after a long run, I visited a hypnotist with a friend named Paula to explore past-life regression, popular at the time. Cleopatra was a no-show, as were peasants and paupers; instead, my mind took me on a journey into cathood. I morphed into a silent, solitary, jungle cat. That is an enduring memory. My house cats seemed oddly gregarious when I arrived home. My sense-of-self was unexpectedly bolstered.

To give my *mind* some playtime, after a long week of mental gymnastics and scientific marathoning, I would reach for my deck of animal cards. After shuffling the deck, I would lay out the cards to see which animals had *messages* for me that week. Accompanying the cards was a book with a sky-blue cover, titled *Medicine Cards: The Discovery of Power Through the Way of the Animals*.[2] The one that spoke to me the loudest was Spider. Oh, the writing in that book! So many messages I needed to hear. Spider encouraged me to write, create, and review, and weave with an ancient alphabet. I love it, today, when actual spiders visit me.

Eight legs, eight eyes. The arrangement of the eyes is one clue to the identity and behavior of the creature who is staring back at you.[3] To name is to know. The two large forward-facing eyes of green lynx spider (*Peucitia viridans*), surrounded by a support system of six, provide a clue to her hunting ability. She is the panther of the spider world, chasing prey at high speeds, leaping across chasm from leaf to leaf. She is one of seventeen species of spiders we have documented in our garden and hopefully not the last. Go, Team Arachnid!

Jumping spiders are hunters, too. One morning, after digging a hole for a plant on which they like to hunt, or so I had read, I stretched out on a porch chair and reached for my deep-blue coffee mug, the one with the turtle emblems. I was about to take a sip of the invigorating liquid when I noticed a jumping spider perched on the handle.

"What are you doing there, little one?" I asked. Her response? She jumped right into my open maw. Talk about putting words in

FIGURE 23 Jumping spider (*Habronattus*) on sacred datura (*Datura wrightii*). Photo by Julie Stromberg.

one's mouth! As she exited, I may have heard her whisper, "We are more alike than different." Maybe so, but you still have more legs than me. *Ptui!*

BASSWOOD: KEEPING A PACT

I use my legs to climb trees to this very day. Or, at least, to yesterday. (But the day is still young . . .) I have no choice. I made a pact.

As a kid in Wisconsin, I couldn't wait for school to let out so I could scramble up the basswood tree (*Tilia americana*) in the side yard or the crab apple (*Malus sylvestris*) in the front yard with an equally arboreal friend named Julie. On the schoolyard itself, we climbed the apple tree during recess until the teacher declared it unsafe and told us to play, instead, on the metal monkey bars over asphalt (!).

It was when I was twenty, and volunteering at the local Audubon center, where Schlitz draft horses once grazed, that I made the pact.

A fellow volunteer named Beth and I were sitting in a tree, I can't remember which species, chatting, bonding, and sharing details of our lives. We vowed to keep climbing trees even when we became very old ladies. So far? I am on track.

It is challenging, though, in a dryland setting, to find or grow trees who are large enough and spineless enough to climb. Many of the velvet mesquites in our woodland have low limbs that sprawl across the ground, but those limbs are well protected. In a burst of frustration, one Saturday morning, I rummaged in the tool shed, found a soft mallet, and began pounding off the sharp bits from the low branches of the oldest and largest velvet mesquite, and the Mexican palo verdes, too. It became an interesting metaphorical exercise in clearing away negative thoughts. And it cleared the way for . . .

Tree-climbing parties! Many urban dwellers have not climbed a tree since childhood. Interesting and intimate conversations ensue. Muscles are stretched that have been on a long vacation. "[T]he biological and adaptive significance of human climbing has been underestimated," with respect to the evolution of our species, and "some humans are surprisingly competent in trees."[4] That would be me! During yesterday's small party, we hung upside down, Karen and I, her long hair dangling free, as her young daughter posed like a leopard. We had an invigorating time in the sturdy, protective branches. It felt like home.

Beth, I hope you are still climbing, too.

RESTORING WALKING TRAILS

PUNCTURE VINE: FREEDOM TO WALK

I love to walk almost as much as I love to run (or climb). When I walk, I think. When our dogs are exploring the garden, they produce a pattern resembling the Lévy walk of foragers: short darts this way and that, with longer-move steps in between.[5] Who knows, maybe our thoughts are stimulated to dart about as we move our bodies around. Physical movement is known to enhance creativity, researchers report; movement—even just squeezing a ball—enhances our cognition and helps our mind *grasp* concepts.[6] Our perspective changes in more ways than one as we hang upside down. Unfortunately, young cities like Phoenix were not designed to be walkable or climbable. Walking has been nearly engineered out of existence in our auto-centric nation and how sad is that.

One weekend, Matt and I flew to San Diego, California, for a family wedding trip and, just for fun, decided to walk across town, not drive, from hotel to beach. What an exercise in madness. We delighted in wildflowers emerging through cracks in the asphalt but were bombarded by vehicular sound waves and immune-suppressing exhaust fumes. At one point, we were scrambling up and over a highway embankment because the sidewalk literally disappeared beneath our feet. Shel Silverstein, I don't think that is *quite* what you meant in your poem "Where the Sidewalk Ends."[7]

Thankfully, today, I don't need to venture *too* far out the gate to find a soft walking path. Aging knees appreciate soft cushion, as do hooves of the horses who amble by on weekends. The Bermuda grass along our verge is remarkably resilient to being trod upon, and the patches of sharp-seeded puncture vines are not that hard to avoid. The pathway that lines the irrigation canal that traverses our South Phoenix neighborhood remains unpaved.[8]

But *damn* it is hot and sunny out there. Not *too* many decades ago, the canals had dirt bottoms, and the Salt River water they were transporting seeped into the soil to feed the roots of the Fremont cottonwoods and other plants who bordered and shaded them. But the riparian thickets were deemed incompatible by the local utility—Salt River Project. They cleared the competing trees so they could have space to string power lines across the valley and to better account for the surface water they were charged with delivering.

Some of Phoenix's canal paths are being revitalized. I hope the trend continues. I hope the revitalizations involve more trees and less concrete. How lovely it would be to remove that concrete liner from the canal and, once again, allow a stately row of riparian trees to grow. How lovely it would be to restore a multifunctional landscape,

one which not only delivers irrigation water but recharges the aquifer, shades the walkers and fishermen, and provides perches for birds
and occasional primates.

How lovely it would it be to have tree-lined walkways accessible
to more than just a privileged few.

BERMUDA GRASS: SOD IS GREAT

I need to take a moment to say I have nothing personal against
sod. It is only that there is so very much of it in our sprawling city.
So many precious resources—water, nutrients, and fossil-fuel—are
diverted from elsewhere to maintain this façade of civilization. Yes,
we can control plants. I get it! But should we? What are we losing
by preventing other plants, be they cinchweed (*Pectis papposa*), dan-
delion (*Taraxacum officinale*), or black medick (*Medicago lupulina*)
from intermingling in the swaths of Bermuda?

The tallgrass prairies of the Midwest, and the shorter ones of
the American Southwest, are not just *grass*lands. In those complex
ecosystems, *Poaceae* coexist with *Fabaceae*, *Asteraceae*, and other
families of plants. Each plant has their own niche—their own root-
ing depth, environmental tolerances, and entourage of organisms.
The collective fixation and storage of carbon, building of soil, and
support of animal life by a diverse community far exceeds that of
any one plant alone.[9]

The fiery skipper (*Hylephila phyleus*) is one who appreciates our
devotion to sod. The caterpillars of these reddish-yellow beauties,
who have been referred to as "the world's most urban butterfly,"
feed on grass, including Bermuda, and one can reliably see them
in parks and yards around our hot city.[10] Cute as they are, they
can become repetitive. Our minds thrive on novelty and diversity.
I, selfishly or not, want to see more than one species of butterfly
when out walking my dog. Yes, sod is great. I bow down to sod,
when doing my yoga. But I am polytheistic when it comes to the
plants. And, really, all we need to do is cut back on the fertilizing, mowing, and herbiciding, and the others will come in on

FIGURE 24 Fiery skipper (*Hylephila phyleus*) nectaring at common lantana (*Lantana camara*). Photo by Julie Stromberg.

their own.[11] Once there, the *Fabaceae*, many of them, will even add nitrogen to the soil, for free.

City dwellers have ancestral roots that reach around the world, and our plants have traveled with us: some we have brought intentionally—those with whom we form mutualisms, and others, the commensals who grow in the habitats we create, have arrived accidentally on our boats, trains, cars, and feet. Some of the plants I have encountered in less kempt lawns, like cinchweed and various euphorbs, are Sonoran regionals. Others, like Bermuda grass, came from afar. And that's okay.

"A strict adherence to a 'pure' native plant landscape, with all of the editing, eradicating, and protecting necessary to preserve it, puts an unnatural construct on nature and natural selection" says the author of the Garden Rant blog.[12] "Reflexive demonization of alien species ignores the beautiful but complex truth that nature fights to find a way—and for a planet navigating the pressures of climate change and overpopulation, that just might be our saving grace."

When we embrace plant diversity in lawns, as many are doing, we send a message of inclusivity that ripples widely. When we stop fixating on the monoculture, we telegraph the message that more than one kind is valued. That the *Poaceae*, as fine as they may be, cushioning our feet and filling our bowls with cereal, are not the only exalted ones in our midst.

Expending energy to suppress diversity is a luxury none can afford.

GETTING LOST

THE DANCING TREE: CONNECTING WITH INDIVIDUALS

Matt has a well-developed mental map and a set of hippocampal place cells to envy.[13] I have been known to become lost in the field, while my mind is elsewhere, focusing on logistics of collecting data instead of, say, on where I parked the car. I occasionally get lost on hiking trails, too, but I have learned, now, to orient when I arrive at a new place: face north to scan the horizon (and stretch upward to connect to the universe; a girl's got to multitask) and then east (scan and stretch), and finally south and west. It seems to be helping.

I lost my way in life, a bit, while being a scientist. In our journey through time, we need to pause, now and then, and reassess, to make sure we are on the path we want to be on. The analytical part of myself was taking center stage, leaving room for little else. I was quantifying and detecting but tamping down emotions to try and remain objective. I was connecting, but not at the level my "soul" needed if I dare venture into that uncharted realm. My path, like that of the channels of the powerful desert rivers I studied, has avulsed. It is time to realign.

In conservation biology, *species* is a primary unit of concern. As a plant ecologist, Arizona eryngo (*Eryngium sparganophyllum*), Huachuca water umbel (*Lilaeopsis schaffneriana spp. recurva*), and other species were the focus of my study.[14] Species are composed of populations, and populations are composed of individuals. We, ourselves, are individuals. At the animal shelter, and in my garden, I find myself relaxing into the pleasure of interacting with other selves. At the shelter, each companion animal has its own name: Oreo, Brownie, Jarabe. Wait, that is my grocery wish list! In our garden, I climb the "Dancing Tree" and the "Magical Conversation" tree. I climb the ones who live long enough to be named. What joy to interact with trees as friends rather than as study organisms. I am reveling in the newfound connections. I like this new path I am on. I will try and tread as softly as I can, with my two very strong legs.

DESERT LARKSPUR: STAYING OBJECTIVE

Periodically during my career, great tears of anguish and despair over the state of the Earth and her inhabitants have escaped my being. Most often, this occurred while in a giant shopping mall or food store, surrounded by "stuff" (and by onlookers, how embarrassing!). Only a few times have I cried similarly great tears of happiness.

That happened most recently one April, soon after my retirement. It had been a difficult year of recovery from a viral illness that intermittently sapped my energy for months. My dog Chip and I had ventured across town to a nature preserve in the high desert hills on the north side of the valley. Rain had fallen again only the day before and the trails were alive with beauty. I was surrounded by plants I knew well and by unfamiliars for whom the hills near our house were too dry.

Well into the day, after chatting with hikers—Chip is a talkative boy—we crossed the flowing creek and rounded the corner into a side canyon. It was spectacularly silent. Wind rustled through the leaves of a lone Fremont cottonwood and honeybees buzzed a white-flowered tamarisk. I glanced to my left and saw a rock wall coated in Arizona wrightwort (*Carlowrightia arizonica*), a plant with flowers as gorgeous as orchids. The hillside to my right was vivid red with chuparosa and hummingbirds. My heart swelled beyond capacity, and tears of gratitude spilled out of my eyes.

After another turn of the trail, I encountered *Delphinium parryi*, also known as desert larkspur. In case you are unfamiliar with her, I will tell you that she is in the buttercup family, has poison that could knock you dead, and sends flowering stalks up from her subterranean bulbs only when she darn well feels like it. She dropped me down to my knees. I am not one who is prone to devotional prayer. That day, I was. Here is what I heard, in the moment we shared: restore the compassion to your words, or their truth will go unheard.

Scientific writing, by definition, is factual. Dry, some say. That is the goal. Over the decades, I had studiously winnowed out the emotion from my words, like chaff from the grain, as well as from those of others, in my role as editor. There is a place for emotion and a place for objective fact. I understand that. But in training the emotion out of my voice, did I drain it out of my deeds? Had I edited it out of my core?

To nurture and protect the plants around us, we must love them. Scientific facts are important. They guide our actions as caretakers of the land. But all the facts in the world won't matter if we haven't formed caring relationships.

It was time, I was reminded, to rejuvenate that which had been dormant too long. Thank you, oracle of delphinium. I will try, as I can, to water my words with joy. Even during the dry spells of despair.

SUNFLOWER: SWAYING IN THE BREEZE

Plants don't get lost. Or run away, like dogs or humans sometimes do. They ever-so-politely stay in one place, so you know where to find them. But plants too, though rooted in space, navigate. More slowly than we, for sure. Plants are alive with motion.

In our garden, I love to walk around and say hello to my plant friends. I receive an oxytocin-type buzz with them, just as I do with the dogs. One of my favorites is sunflower. Look at that phototropic girl now, spiraling ever so slowly to the east, toward the light, while

FIGURE 25 Annual sunflower (*Helianthus annuus*) reaching for the light. Photo by Matt Chew.

politely accounting for her neighbors' leaves. I had a moment with her, yesterday. I entered her world, briefly, and felt myself gently swaying in the wind and bobbing as the bees and bee-mimics alit. "*Me, me, land on me*," I heard the collective yearning, the need intensified by the waning summer days.

Behind her, I saw the tendrils of blue passionflower (*Passiflora caerulea*) slow-scrambling up the trellis, tying themselves in knots. Over in the meadow, the chemotropic seedlings of field dodder (*Cuscuta campestris*) were finding their way in the world by seeking the volatiles that guide them to the host plant who helped birth them.[15] Oops . . . careful, don't dance to close to chainfruit cholla (*Cylindropuntia fulgida*)! She has a bad case of the glochids, and those barbed spines hurt when you extract them from flesh. Stand back and imagine her roots, after yesterday's rain, growing toward the sound of water. I wonder what she hears.

Inside their bodies, plants are as fast-moving as we. Action potentials zip quickly from cell to cell. And a few shining stars have

10

TROPHIC DYNAMICS

What's Eating You?

PLANTS AND HERBIVORES

WHY IS THE WORLD GREEN?

"WHAT ARE you barking at, silly dog?" Chip threw a quick glance my way and then continued his vocal assault on the ... cows? Our next-door neighbor has cows? And a bull? They were as unexpected to me as they were to the barky boy. "Thanks, Chip, for the warning. They certainly are big, but they don't pose a danger, at least not to us."

There are no plant-munching bovines on our side of the fence, but there are plenty of rabbits. Desert cottontails are here by the dozen. Our pack of four dogs—and the occasional coyote—can't keep pace with the fecund bunnies. As a result, some of our lovely plants are munched to bits.

Over half a century ago, a trio of ecologists wrote a paper asking, "Why is the world green?"[1] They discussed the influence on vegetation of bottom-up processes, such as soil nutrients and water, and of top-down processes, such as herbivory. They asked, why don't the animals eat the plants into oblivion? The simplified answer is this: carnivores keep the herbivores in check. When carnivores increase, herbivores decrease, allowing the plants to thrive. When herbivores are abundant, more plants are consumed. The poorly protected ones, anyway. They are replaced by a new suite of plants who are spinier or packed with more poison. An abundance of herbivores can overwhelm some plants' capacity for defense.

Trophic cascade is the term that refers to these suites of changes.[2] The term conjures, in my mind, the sound of water gushing over rocks. The reality is not always so pleasant. To assist the unprotected, and halt the local cascade, we enclose small patches of our garden in rabbit-proof fence.

Chip's barky outburst raises an interesting question: if you found yourself in danger, what would you do? Would you holler like Mr. Chip? Would you run? Or spray capsaicin at your assailant? Let's make this more challenging. If you were a *plant*, and found yourself in danger, what would you do?[3] Defend your tissues with poisons? Grow a set of spines? If you were lucky enough to live in the rich part of town, might you eschew such protections and simply regrow from reserves as needed?

Velvet mesquite, a predominant tree in our woodland, has gone the mechanical route. She grows large thorns to deter the large mammals, such as those cows next door, who would eat her nutritious leaves. I had an "aha" moment regarding her capacity for self-defense, early in my career. It happened while a graduate student and I were visiting a mesquite bosque in southern Arizona. Our goal was to help a land protection group restore the plant communities on their riparian preserve. The understory vegetation had been altered by over-stocked cows, and the woodland was now carpeted by annual grasses with very sharp awns—the poorly defended had been replaced. The preserve manager drew our attention to a well-armed mesquite, while delivering a revelation to me and the aptly named Barb. "Look at those thorns!" we gasped. They were, indeed, larger than usual. More than an inch long and thick. The revelation? That the tree, in response to injury, had upgraded her thorns.

As we leaned in to take another look, a spine poked Barb's finger. She let out a yip and jerked back. The neurons in her digit alerted her system to mobilize a response. Thank goodness for pain. The mesquite tree, too, had mobilized a response, sending signals within her body that warned: we've been harmed. She, who could not fight or flee, communicated her distress elsewise. The tree couldn't walk away as we did, but she could grow bigger thorns for next time. We reported our findings on the understory to the land protection group and, also, internalized this message: when plants speak to us, we need to listen. We need to at least try to understand. When we receive signals of overgrazing, we should get our cows the "heifer out of there" and move them to greener pastures.

It is exciting to be alive in this era of scientific discovery about the myriad ways that plants communicate—electrical signals, chemicals flowing through the root zone or soaring through the air—and revel in the finding of those at the leading edge of research. It is steadying to be a part of the knowledge cascade, sharing flows of information to those in need.

DESERT TOBACCO: UP IN SMOKE

There is so much desert tobacco (*Nicotiana obtusifolia*) in our garden! She grows along the trails and in them. She, with desert senna, is one of our most common herbaceous wildlings. She is a dominant species in ecology-speak. Like many in our harsh climate, she thrives in partial shade, but she owes much of her local success to her capacity to outwit the rabbits. They eat the unprotected plants with whom she competes for space. Nicotine-filled leaves are not a preferred item on the rabbits' menu.

Desert tobacco is smart. At first perceived munch, she ramps up production of her expensive chemical deterrents, to protect her tissues from future harm.[4] The rabbits, in turn, learn not to ingest her. Other plants have learned to increase the density of their protective hairs, or trichomes, after being eaten by insect or mammal. Such responses can be taxa specific. They are known in the botanical world as induced defenses, being somewhat analogous to our immune response to pathogens.[5]

I wish my mother had taken a cue from the rabbits' play book. My mother was a smoker, having fallen victim to powerful nicotine marketing.[6] Nicotine-filled leaves went up in smoke and into her lungs for far too many years. Her heart gave out in her sixties, some twenty years after giving birth to her children. Short women have more cardiac difficulties than taller ones, I have read, and I believe it was a lifetime of stress, and smoking to cope with that stress, that did her in. The self-confidence of that young artist had been shattered early in life, she told us. That natural lefty, who loved to draw pictures of plants, was told as a schoolchild she must conform to the norm and learn to write with her right. What an archaic practice. She was not a confident woman, and lived, it seemed, in the shadow of a promiscuous husband. The garden was where she blossomed.

Four decades ago, I was vacationing in the North Woods of Wisconsin when I received a phone call that nearly dropped *me* dead in my tracks. Her heart had failed. For weeks after, I picked at my food, ran trails burning tears as fuel, and dropped into anorexia zone. I was untethered. She was my caregiver, and I was not ready. Death of one's mother when you are not quite a woman influences the way you interact with the world. You become independent quickly and grateful for what you still have. Finally, one day, I dreamed of a rose, a beautiful rose emerging from the ashes. I called my brother to tell him, calmed down, and readjusted (some of) my life choices. Darn, I still miss her.

I'm glad wild tobacco found our garden. I like her. I like to look at her and admire her intelligence and beauty. I remain grateful for learning not to inhale her chemicals into my lungs.

DEVIL'S CLAW: PROTECTING HERSELF

"[He has] an inordinate fondness for beetles."[7] When asked by a theologian what one could conclude about the nature of the Creator based on a study of his creation, that is what the neo-Darwinian J. B. S. Haldane allegedly replied. Beetles *are* a species-rich group. In our garden, so far, we have seen twenty-nine species in the order of beetles—the Coleopterans—including the emerald-green figeaters (*Cotinus mutabilis*) who lay eggs in our mulch piles. But they better get hopping, or crawling or flying, because the order of true bugs, the Hemipterans, at forty-four taxa, has surpassed them: hackberry psylloids (*Leuronota maculata*), mesquite choreids (*Mozena arizonensis*), redcoat seed bugs (*Melanopleurus belfragei*), .. so many to count!

Despite all the herbivores, the plants in the orchard don't need our assistance in the form of chemical baths. Thanks in part to the messiness of my gardening style (in keeping with my housekeeping style—sorry Mom), the six-legged and eight-legged predators who feed on the bugs that munch on the leaves and suck at the stems are diverse and abundant. Green lacewings (*Chrysoperla* sp.) and leaf-hopper assassin bugs (*Zelus renardii*) are *everywhere*, mantids and katydids bless us with their presence now and then, and the larval stages of aphid-eater flies are true to their name. Convergent lady beetles (*Hippodamia convergens*) rest in the cupped leaves of wild lettuce and sow thistles (*Sonchus* spp.), who I am training myself not to weed; the pull for purity and order can be strong. Our "natural" predators are doing their jobs.

Remarkably enough? Some of the plants are killers themselves. The plant called devil's claw (*Proboscidea parviflora*), or *ihug* in O'odham culture, can help with small-insect control when planted near other plants.[8] She is a protocarnivore.[9] A flypaper plant. Tiny insects become trapped in the sticky mucilage of her glandular hairs, and large bugs who can negotiate her foliar landscape arrive to feed on the bodies. The excrement from these predators fertilizes the plants, causing ecologists to regurgitate the term "digestive mutualism" to describe the nature of this plant-insect relationship.

I love devil's claw! One of our neighbors to the north, an engineer-turned-organic-farmer after a life-changing epiphany, recently planted an orchard. After the irrigation water began flowing, an amazing suite of plants emerged from the soil seed bank, devil's claw among them. She is going wild in the water and heat. I have never seen her in such abundance. Thankfully, our neighbor welcomes her in the understory.

His orchard, and our garden, host other protocarnivores, too. What a surprise! I have seen small wasps die while trying to escape the mucilaginous clutches of red spiderling (*Boerhavia coccinea*) and I have watched as flies succumb to the glandular trichomes of a plant you met earlier, camphorweed. The wild leadwort (*Plumbago zeylanica*) we planted, it turns out, ensnares ants with her sticky parts, and may, in fact, release enzymes, proteases, to digest them. It is sad to see the insects struggling but, I suppose, that is life in the big city. The big city garden, that is.

The Creator, it seems, also has an inordinate fondness for mucilage. That's just as *catchy* a quote, don't you think?

SUBSIDIZED PROTECTION

GOOSEFOOT: ONE FOOT IN THE PAST

A field trip is afoot! My friend Liz and I were invited to a wholesaler's garden for a private tour. There are benefits to being notorious plant nerds in a neighborhood filled with farmers.

Once there, we met the owner, a fifth-generation farmer who has "never not had a garden," in his words. His approach to surviving as a small farmer in the world of corporate conglomerates is grounded in the concept of bet-hedging. He has embraced diversity at the spatial scale and has a continental reach: a family farm in the Midwest (with walnut trees), a ranch in the Arizona highlands (with twenty-three species of grass), and irrigated acreage in South Phoenix to supply desert trees and showy flowers to residents of the Valley (and to grow a passel of veggies). If one farm locale struggles, the others will thrive and carry it through. This "don't put all your eggs in one basket" approach to risk has served him well.

A recent graduate from Arizona State University is the main grower. After gasping in delight at the magnificent shade on her globemallow (*Sphaeralcea* sp.) flowers (how to describe it . . . scarlet iris red, if one relies on *Werner's Nomenclature of Colours*, or razzmatazz, if one matches to Crayola crayons), we walked into one of the shaded grow-houses. There, we discussed the uptick in business driven by COVID-quarantined plant-seekers and oohed and aahed over baby cacti who will produce night-blooming flowers with heavenly scents. After dodging the tower of commercial bags of mycorrhizal fungi on the way out, we proceeded to the vegetable garden, of which she was clearly proud. It was gorgeous and bountiful. The two of them filled bags with yellow beets (*Beta vulgaris*), white cauliflower (*Brassica oleracea*), and deep green spinach (*Spinacia oleracea*) for us to take home. As we took one last look at the garden, the owner apologized for the few weeds between the neat rows. I looked down to see who he was pointing at and was heartened to see nettle-leaved goosefoot (*Chenopodiastrum murale*). The close relatives of this little chenopod were part of the diet of early Europeans, back in the Mesolithic, some 15,000 years ago, and she, herself, is edible.[10] These chenopods have been transported with us, as we farmed new lands, and this commensal partnership could become mutualistic again.

The owner views them as competitors, though, in his quest to maximize productivity of the plantings. He was influenced by the green revolution of the 1950s and 1960s, also called the third agricultural revolution. He vividly recalled hearing a talk by one its central figures, Norman Borlaug, born the same year as my mother, 1914. The essence of the revolution was this: a small number of strains of genetically identical crops were bred to channel their energy into their edible parts. Their own capacity for defense against herbivores and tolerance of drought and other stressors was bred out and replaced by subsidies of fossil-fuel biocides, fertilizer, and water. Many hailed the global expansion of the industrial farms and their high productivity, yet there were, and are, costs. Indigenous farming, as practiced mostly by women, was ramrodded nearly out of existence.[11] Centuries of place-based knowledge were eroded, along with the local soils and plants themselves.

Using long-stored energy to fuel the present growth of crops is not without risk. This chenopod is a link to the past. We may need this little plant again, and the edible botanical diversity she so resolutely represents. Plant productivity increases with species diversity, to a point, especially when averaged across time.[12] One plant may be highly productive in a dry year, and another species in a wetter year; each has their moment to shine. Maintaining botanical links to our ancestral foods is conceptually like the owner's "multiple basket" approach to succeeding in business; it is a means of buffering the risk. If the canals go dry, or fossil fuels become too costly, we may need self-sufficient plants to carry us through.

As we said our final goodbyes, I heard the main grower whisper, in an offside to the wind, "I prefer it a bit messier." She was referring, of course, to the garden and revealing a difference in their styles. Yes, listen to the wind, I thought. And keep one foot planted in the past, to provide options for the future.

OKRA-Y BY ME

No, it's not okay. It's slimy! What am I talking about? Okra (*Abelmoschus esculentus*). If you are an okra lover, you probably like nopales, too. Not me. Too much mucilage. I suppose I am missing out an abundance of healthy fiber by eschewing these lovely members of the mallow and cactus families, but that's okay. There are many other options.

There are benefits to having a diversity of foods to select from. And if you are *growing* food, there are benefits to filling your fields with multiple species of plants as opposed to just one.[13] In a farm in central Mexico, yield and water use were found to differ between a monoculture of maize (*Zea mays*) and a triculture of maize, faba bean (*Vicia faba*) and squash (*Cucurbita moschata*).[14] Yield of the maize was greater in the triculture because the other plants provided habitat for lady beetles and other predaceous insects. Water use was more efficient in the triculture because less water was evaporating from the shaded soils. If you want to be productive *and* efficient as a farmer, diversity is your friend.

One of the most plant-diverse spaces in our South Phoenix neighborhood, at least with respect to the edible kind, is the community garden called Spaces of Opportunity. This lovely multiacre patch, surrounded by suburbia, makes the term biocultural diversity come to life. When I trot up to there with my camera, to see ~~what~~ who is new, I am never disappointed. Many cultures are represented in the farm plots, thus there are many species of edible plants. One can see taro (*Colocasia esculenta*) and moringa (*Moringa oleifera*) from Asia, sesame (*Sesamum* sp.) and watermelon (*Citrullus lanatus*) from Africa, and tomatillo (*Physalis* sp.) and nopal (*Opuntia* spp.) from the Americas. Fields of giant sunflowers abut border strips planted for pollinators. The plethora of plants support a rich mix of pollinating insects and predacious ones, too.

Some farmers are planting landraces, and in so doing helping to maintaining diversity *within* species. Many of the sowing mixes are genetically diverse, with each seed having slightly different strengths and weaknesses than their siblings, maintaining diversity within populations. Some new farmers are struggling, as one does in new ventures when links to the past have been severed: the learning curve is steep. But there is a sense of community, connection, and joy.

We have lost our way, a bit, as a society. Our relationship with the plants who feed us needs repair.[15] Community gardens such as

FIGURE 26 Oblique longhorn bee (*Svastra obliqua*) nectaring at sunflower (*Helianthus* sp.) at Spaces of Opportunity community garden. Photo by Julie Stromberg.

Spaces of Opportunity are a pathway to healing. There are other such places in the region. Maya's Farm in South Phoenix is emblematic of the rise in women farmers who are embracing organic agriculture. The Ajo Center for Sustainable Agriculture, southwest of Phoenix, is evidence of the revitalization of traditional ecological knowledge held by displaced Indigenous peoples.

South Phoenix is in desperate need of green places of healing. South Phoenix has a long history of being on the wrong side of the tracks and of the (once) wildly flooding Salt River. Anglos settled on the north, and Latinos, African Americans, and other disenfranchised groups settled on the south. Spaces of Opportunity is but one of many small urban farms and gardens that are springing back to life on the rich Rillito loam, creating a patchwork of verdant diversity at the landscape scale. And that's okay by me.

Okra? You really like that stuff? And let's not even get into the cilantro (*Coriandrum sativum*) debate![16]

CARNIVORES AND OMNIVORES

LIVING WITH OUTDOOR CATS

Domesticated felines make fine companions. I have befriended my share over the years. Not lately though. Our current pack of dogs—one in particular—ahem, Ms. Sunshine—has made her feelings on the matter well known. She has a zero-tolerance policy. Should a stray cat wander onto our acreage, I regret to say, they may not wander out. They may find themselves up a tree until we can put the pack inside, giving them a chance to flee. To those neighbors whose cats have unknowingly crossed into our territory, I issue a heartfelt apology.

Free-roaming cats (*Felis catus*) in the city foster strong opinions. Some worry, understandably, about the birds that are being killed.[17] Others applaud their killing of roof rats (*Rattus rattus*). Ecologists sifting through studies on wildlife survival in cities have come to an interesting conclusion. They have noted the existence of a predation paradox: in urban areas, compared to rural, there often are more predators but lower rates of local predation.[18] Some rabbits and birds, when living in cities, have *higher* survivorship than their counterparts in rural areas and become less fearful of being eaten. This phenomenon is called predation relaxation which, honestly, makes me want to stop and take a catnap right about now.

But the cats are calling. Caterwauling, even! The trophic reach of our domesticated cats, much like the sound of their mating, is expansive. Their predation occurs locally—in one's backyards—as well as, by proxy, across the globe.[19] The extruded kibbles in the bowls of our neighbors' cats were, at one time, sardines or herrings swimming in the ocean before being caught in a net, processed in a factory, and shipped across country. What a life of luxury cats live. They farm out their killing to us and then turn up their nose at our offerings.

Domestic cats are classified as mesopredators: they are smaller than cougars (*Puma concolor*) but similar in size to the gray foxes (*Urocyon cinereoargenteus*) who we rarely see because they are as sly as . . . well, you know. A small population of gray fox lives on the campus of Arizona State University, a surprisingly green space that supports an arboretum. One member of the campus gray fox population gained infamy by being captured on film dashing across a football field during a game: "Look at this speed! Look at this dexterity! It darted around the field, leaped into the stands, then got out of the end zone and eventually dashed out of a tunnel, and hopefully it's safe and OK after a harrowing experience," commented one reporter.[20]

I, too, hope the gray fox was safe. Life in a city is difficult enough as a human. Hmm . . . foxes eat rabbits . . . maybe we should take a cue from Michael Rosenzweig's book *Win-Win Ecology: How the Earth's Species Can Survive in the Midst of Human Enterprise* and build the foxes a den?[21] So many decisions. So many questions.

Trophic dynamics, like life itself, are complicated.

RATS!

"Rats." *What's the matter, dear?* "Rats!" *I know you are upset, but about what?* "There's a *rat* in the car again!" *Ohhh!*

We don't have as many as we did a few months ago, though. The drinkable birth control is working. It must be tasty. Or perhaps, having run out of citrus to eat, the roof rats (*Rattus rattus*) are desperately hungry. It's not that I don't like these small mammals—they are not that different from the Syrian hamsters (*Mesocricetus auratus*) my brother and I played with as children. But I don't like the damage they do when they burrow in insulation or chew on wires. Our dog Chip alerts us to their presence—he loves the chase—but he can't clamber around in small spaces to dispatch them. That is why we need a rat terrier. Maybe I should dash up to the shelter and adopt ~~one~~ two!

Someday. For now, we rely on the liquid bait, as the company calls their product. It contains two active ingredients: one targets the motility of the sperm, and the other is lethal to the eggs of the rats. The birth control is "equal opportunity" which is something that we can't yet say about methods for our own species. The motility reducer, exciting enough to this botanist, is produced by a plant called thunder god vine (*Tripterygium wilfordii*).[22] She sounds powerful! The vine, which is a member of the *Celastraceae* family, has a long history of medicinal use in China. Many traditional medicines have yet to be subject to rigorous Western-medicine-style testing for efficacy, but the number is growing each year. The liquid contraceptive is a fine alternative to setting out lethal poison for adult rats and, thus, for protecting the nontarget rodents and the owls and hawks who might eat them.

In our four acres, over the years, we have shared space with over a dozen members of Class Mammalia, many within Order Rodentia. Yesterday, we looked out the back window and saw a family of Arizona cotton rats (*Sigmodon arizonae*)—a mother and four babies—happily munching on the greenery. Merriam's kangaroo rat (*Dipodomys merriami*), rock pocket mouse (*Chaetodipus intermedius*), rock squirrel (*Osteospermophilus variegatus*), and woodrat (*Neotoma* sp.) also made it onto the list. We have yet to see a black-tailed jackrabbit (*Lepus californicus*) but no one place can have them all. That would be a zoo! We occasionally put wire mesh around

FIGURE 27 Arizona cotton rat (*Sigmodon arizonae*) nibbling the vegetation. Photo by Matt Chew.

the root ball of companion plants, so they won't be munched by the gophers, but that seems a small price to pay to coexist with one's neighbors.

My favorites of the bunch are the round-tailed ground squirrels who scamper about with their long tails projected expertly into in the air. So cute! Most of the year, they are sensibly ensconced in their burrows, staying warm or cool, depending on season, but come spring we see them darting about. In summer, after the fruit of velvet mesquite have ripened, we know they have entered the above-ground world as evidenced by the distinctive pattern of tooth marks on the discarded pods.

As much as I love squirrels, my love pales in comparison to one of Matt's friends. This friend has inveigled himself into the hearts of a community of rock squirrels who live in a park near his home. He knows the squirrels by name and rescues them from dangers, such as floods. He visits them regularly to feed them and film them. Just now, how's that for synchronicity, Matt came dashing up the stairs asking, "How many almonds can a rock squirrel fit in her cheek pouches?" his friend having sent a video of a happy squirrel and some nuts (or maybe of a happy nut and some squirrels?). The answer is thirty in case it arises on trivia night. For bonus points, pecans are preferred over almonds (*Prunus amygdalus*).

"Rats!" *Now what's wrong?* "I guessed forty-two." No trivia prize for me.

SNAKES ON A PLAIN

The snake experts in the Valley tell us we are lucky. We agree. We saw a western gopher snake (*Pituophis catenifer*) early on but the snake population in our garden now consists exclusively of California kingsnakes (*Lampropeltis californiae*). These constrictor-type beauties were crowned as royalty because, as royals will do, they eat the competition.[23] As in eating diamondback rattlers (*Crotalus atrox*), the other large snake we might commonly see. The kingsnakes also eat lizards and eggs as well as a baby rat or two. Kingsnakes have a docile nature and are commonly kept as pets by herpetophiles. I am grateful for the wild ones.

The young snakes are adorable! Matt's eye for pattern allows him to distinguish individuals based on variation in their black and white color bands. We know they are breeding on our property because we caught them in the act. I spent part of one morning watching through the window as two of them coiled into each other. They had conveniently selected a secluded spot under the mountain laurel that was visible from the living room couch. The narration wasn't as scintillating as on the wildlife shows my generation grew up on but at least the acting wasn't staged.

I worry more about our dogs harming these wild creatures than the other way around. The "leave it" command, as learned in doggy obedience school, works well in these situations, especially if we see the snake before the dog does. If one desires more specialized training for their dogs, snake aversion classes are available, though the methods used by some, such as shock collars, make me cringe. I occasionally see a rattlesnake in the nearby desert preserve and respectfully keep my distance. I don't worry too much, though, because I am not in the demographic most likely to be bitten: rattlesnake bites are "most common in young men who often are intoxicated and have purposely handled a venomous snake."[24] That is not me!

Decades ago, one of my young female dogs had an unfortunate encounter with a rattlesnake. The telltale fang marks were clearly visible. We rushed to the nearest emergency clinic, way across town, to receive a shot of antivenin. Thankfully, Sierra recovered, but I'm certain the experience was not pleasant for her or, for that matter, for the snake who had to be milked to collect the venom which would be injected into the sheep or horse from whom blood would be extracted and fractionated.

And that, my friends, is the main reason I am grateful to the kingsnakes. Go ahead, eat the competition. Put the squeeze on them. Keep our lucky streak going.

II

CHANGING TIMES

CHANGING THE WEATHER

HUMMINGBIRD HEAT INDEX

"THE HUMMINGBIRD Heat Index is at *thirteen*," Matt declared as he came in from the porch, shutting the door quickly behind. Matt's index is highly localized. It can't be found in the climate books. As the temperature rises, he has observed, the number of hummingbirds perched on the porch trellis, close to the water drip, increases in tandem. Today is the hottest day of summer so far, 113°F, and Matt counted thirteen of the tiny birds! During cooler parts of the year, the hummers are spatially dispersed and squabbling for territory. Now? Surviving is all-consuming.

The "future" is here, sooner than we thought. The projections of the climate models and the reports of the Intergovernmental Panel on Climate Change and are to be ignored at our peril.[1] The reality of the lectures I delivered on climate change are no fun to live through. Triple-digit temperatures in the subtropical Sonoran are becoming as common as ticks on a street dog, and the heat waves are arriving earlier, soaring higher, and lasting longer. Intensification, some call it. High-pressure systems stall above, ratcheting the air to 110°F and above for days at a time. Timing, magnitude, duration, and

frequency of temperature and rainfall are all changing. We have no
one to blame but ourselves. The asphalt and concrete surfaces of the
built environment only exacerbate, raising nighttime temperatures
in particular.[2]

Oh-my-goddess it's hot! If only people had heeded the advice
of the scientists, early on. "Women have been making significant
contributions to science for centuries and receiving little to no credit
for their work" begins an article about Eunice Newton Foote who,
in 1856, one hundred years before I was born, demonstrated that
increase in carbon dioxide leads to atmospheric warming.[3] Her
work was presented at a conference of the American Advancement
of Sciences by a *male* scientist. Another prescient individual warned,
in 1912, about the effects of burning coal and releasing long-stored
carbon into circulation.[4] They and more recent climate scientists
would be angry and frustrated, I imagine, at being ignored.

"Air-conditioning is the best thing ever invented," I heard an
animal-cruelty investigator exclaim, with relief, as they came into
the shelter from the mind-melting heat. But for those who must
stay outside—be they dogs chained in backyards, utility workers
repairing power lines, or birds with mouth agape—the conditioned
air is a pipe dream. Heat is a force to be reckoned with. It adds a
layer of complexity to our behavior. The hotter it gets, the crankier
we get. Small irritants we brush off like gnats, in spring, escalate
to hornets in summer. As it heats up, we are more likely to engage
in violent and aggressive behavior.[5] A study conducted right here
in Phoenix showed that drivers honk their horns more when it is
hot.[6] Even dogs are more likely to bite, as the temperatures warm,
with males particularly prone. We had a power outage not long ago,
and we whooshed into survival mode. Without air-conditioning, or
shade, creatures die.

"But it's a dry heat," people say about our climate. Yes, that
holds true in May and June—they are a time of low humidity in
Phoenix—but July and August, and increasingly September and
October, are hot and humid. Our capacity to self-cool diminishes
under such conditions: the Heat Index developed by Robert G.

Steadman accounts for temperature and humidity and is important for assessing climate livability.[7] I doubt the Hummingbird Heat Index will gain such widespread use, but, to us, it is a reminder that not everyone can come in and cool down.

CHINABERRY: A SOLID AND HELPFUL CITIZEN

Before we purchased our two-story Spanish colonial, its tenants were derelict in their duties. Rock pigeons, rock squirrels, roadrunners, and coyotes were among those who squatted there, for a year, without performing basic maintenance or irrigating the orchard trees. Nor did anyone else. One tree who did survive was chinaberry (*Melia azedarach*), near the leakiest part of the irrigation system. Maybe I am biased—the Mahogany family have a reputation as solid and helpful citizens—but I liked those trees from the start. There was that peculiar incident involving Alfie, our blue merle cattle dog, and the vet. Alfie had gorged on her fallen berries—technically, drupes—and become inebriated, but our country-style doctor advised him to sleep it off and all would be well. Which it was. Other than that, chinaberry has indeed proven helpful. Besides providing perches for western kingbirds and entertaining us with percussion music when she drops her drupes on the metal roof, she is a warrior in the "battle" against the rapidly changing climate. I should have led with that; it is so important.

Air temperature within our hot city can vary from one neighborhood to another by more than ten degrees Fahrenheit depending on the density of trees. The trees are not equitably distributed; the wealthier neighborhoods have denser canopy.[8] To empirically determine how much relief our forest provides, I bought an infrared sensor and was having great fun taking the temperatures of plants in our garden, and of bare ground, too. The temperature was *twenty degrees* lower in the chinaberry/cottonwood patch! You can *feel* the temperature drop when you walk into the woodland, and you can *see* how the leafy branches shade us from solar rays, but what my new toy confirmed was that each living plant, be she tree, shrub, or herb, is cooling the air through a process invisible to our eyes. Even the layer of dead annuals, left over from last year, buffers the temperature for those living in the soil underneath.

My favorite subject in school was not thermodynamics, but for some reason the concept of *latent heat of vaporization* thrills me to the core. The notion of a water molecule transitioning from fluid to gas, and cooling the air in the process, seems like a gift from the gods. Chinaberry and her large-leaved friends cottonwood, elderberry, and velvet ash (*Fraxinus velutina*) transpire gallons of fluid over a course of a day, cooling us and connecting us to the mountains afar. A flake of snow that landed in the White Mountains, say, wended its way into an aquifer and now finds its way skyward in a xylem stream that extends from chinaberry's root to her leaf. As chinaberry opens the little pores in her leaves—the stomates—the water exits, transitioning from liquid to gas and cooling the air in the process. Carbon dioxide enters her body through these same little 'mouths,' and she fixes the carbon into sugars and then sequesters some into yet more complex compounds, helping minimize the atmospheric greenhouse effect and delaying, incrementally, the warming. Shade, evaporative cooling, and carbon sequestration: a three-for-one deal that's hard to pass up.

There are more than 300 trees in our forest garden. I just got back from counting them. It was a quick and dirty count, as it is very hot; I will conduct a more accurate survey come winter. Some of the trees are American in origin; others evolved elsewhere. Certain leaf traits are known to allow for greater capture of carbon and greater transpiration, and these traits do not differ inherently between those classed as aliens vs. natives.[9] All are playing a role. Our tree density is on par with that of John Marzluff, the author of *Welcome to Subirdia*, who went to the trouble of estimating the carbon storage in his forest *and* calculating his household carbon use to arrive at this conclusion: "Our yard is a carbon sink!"[10] I am guessing our yard is, too.

Look for the helpers, they say. She is one. Chinaberry is our refuge in the summer heat.

BRITTLEBUSH: WE ALL HAVE OUR LIMITS

Ecosystem services is not the phrase I would have settled on, had I been on a committee tasked with naming the collective benefits provided by a plant community and her entourage.[11] It is not the most respectful way to refer to the cumulative actions of the plants, fungi, and flies that benefit us. It is a self-centered way to express our gratitude: "What have you done for me lately, ecosystem?" Yet, it is serviceable enough. Aesthetics are no small part of the equation. Matt and I are thrilled when neighbors who are walking down the street slow down to admire sacred datura. "What is that gorgeous plant?" some ask. It is a blissful moment of shared appreciation. Someday, a girl can hope, someone will ask, "*Who* is that gorgeous plant?" and I will jump for joy.

But we must put Beauty, aside, for the moment, and return to the Beast. The relentless dry heat is knocking. At first, when I open the door, the heat embraces, like a lovely sauna. Mmm. But the hot winds pummel like a blast furnace, and back inside I go.

Let's try again.

Back outside, at noon, on this July day, the temperature already in the one-hundreds, I am scouting to see who is up-and-about in the unirrigated part of the garden. Brittlebush (*Encelia farinosa*), semi drought-deciduous shrub that she is, has shut down, her leaves hanging low. As regional temperatures and water stress have increased, she has kept pace: she fixes more carbon per unit of water than she once did, raising her water-use efficiency even higher, but we all have our limits.[12] Creosote, her evergreen buddy, has the anatomical and physiological capacity to keep transforming light into matter in hot and dry conditions but is looking peaked and pale herself. You go, girl! Yes, the heat addles our brain.

The vegetation in the Sonoran Desert ecoregion is changing as the climate warms and becomes more variable.[13] Populations of plant species are moving their ranges upwards on the Santa Catalina Mountains, near Tucson, and presumably on other mountains, as well. Some plants are flowering earlier. The desert vegetation in some areas is becoming sparser, satellite images show. I, myself, witnessed the deaths of creosote bush and buckhorn cholla (*Cylindropuntia acanthocarpa*) at South Mountain Park after a recent hot and dry year. The shrubs in our garden, and the desert hills beyond, with their adaptations for extremes, their collective diversity of temporal and spatial niches, and their partnership with the fungi below, play their part in sequestering carbon and regulating climate. They are helpers, too. Sadly, desert plant communities continue to be destroyed as urban and suburban development spread across the local terrain: "an acre of desert land per hour every hour of every day" is not a welcome thought.[14]

It has been months since the last rain. The summer monsoons are late. We are all getting stressed. You can imagine how relieved we all are, brittlebush included, when the monsoons finally arrive. "At your service," the luscious drops seem to say.

TROPICALIZATION

ARIZONA POPPY: THE RAINS CAME

Drip. Drip. Drip. "UR-a-Ro-Roo!" *What's that, Mak? What's on the roof?* The rain! The rain is on the roof? Yes! We made it through June, perilously hot and dry June, and now the rains are here. It is *finally* wet! The winds, this July afternoon, bring life-giving drops from the south. We are so happy, dancing even, at the sudden downburst. Even the toads, the Couch's spadefoots (*Scaphiopus couchii*), have dug to the surface, entranced by the rumbles and drums. And look! A Colorado River toad (*Incilius alvarius*), on the porch. Did you really emerge from the irrigation pipe? That's a tight squeeze!

We get *drunk* in the water, aa-rooing at the pummeling hail. Ouch! Moments later? *Petrichor.* The smell of the earth after rain. I love that word. We tuck noses into creosote, taking deep whiffs, her protective oils having volatilized into magical goodness. Oh, what's that other smell? *Canichor.* It's not a word but it should be. The smell of wet dog.

FIGURE 28 Seedlings of warm-season annuals pushing through the earth. Photo by Julie Stromberg.

After the rain comes the seedlings. The brave summer annuals, the ones who have been in the soil, like the toads, awaiting the heat and the wet, are dressed up in their fantastical coats. Lookin' good, honeysweet (*Tidestromia lanuginosa*). Who knew that candelabras of multi-branched trichomes were back in style? Nice way to shield yourself from the rays of the sun. Arizona poppy (*Kallstroemia grandiflora*)—your oranges are so *intense!* And our friend brittle-bush has come back to life. What a flexible shrub she is: the hotter it is, the longer and denser she grows the hairs on her leaves.[15] Long and thick in summer, short and sparse in winter and spring. The opposite of me.

The monsoon rains of 2021 were epic. Six whole inches for the season near our house, and evenly spaced. During the two years before that, the recording stations averaged an inch or less. *Non-soons*, they called them. The epic rains turned the desert shrub-lands into grasslands. Six-weeks grama (*Bouteloua barbata*) and three-awns (*Aristida* spp.) carpeted the soil of South Mountain Park, sharing space with knee-high fringed amaranth (*Amaranthus fimbriatus*) and spiderlings (*Boerhavia* spp.). Desert dodder (*Cuscuta tuberculata*) was piled on top, coating the others with her yellow stems. A kaleidoscope of butterflies, American snouts, pygmy blues, and painted ladies among them, feasted on the nectar. The desert was a patchwork of color.

Each season, and each year, is different. The temporal dance carries on. I delight in observing and interpreting the botanical changes around me. To borrow the words of Janice Bowers, one *can* live a full life in a small place.[16] It is good practice for keeping one's carbon footprint small.

Come on monsoons . . . see if you can top 2021!

STRAWBERRY TREE: TROPICAL DELIGHTS

I don't travel on airplanes anymore. I did my fair share of flying to conferences and tag-a-long vacationing over the years and over the planet, but I am through. My reasons are self-protective: too much stress on my body and brain, too much risk of spreading and catching disease, and too much expelling of climate-changing exhaust by the engines. Instead? If I want to go, say, to the tropics? I visit Shamus O'Leary's tropical garden just down the road. Shade cloth covers the garden, serving as surrogate canopy for Barbados cherry (*Malpighia emarginata*), strawberry tree (*Muntinga calubra*), and other nutritious edibles and medicinals who are out of their climatic range.

Or are they? Winter frost, to which these tropical plants are unaccustomed, has become less common in our region, especially in heat-dome cities.[17] The southern tier of the United States is tropicalizing, and tropical plants are inching northward. Some biologists react in horror to such botanical changes, blaming Brazilian pepper tree (*Schinus terebinthifolia*) and other creeping beauties for "altering native plant communities by displacing native species, changing community structures or ecological functions, or hybridizing with natives."[18] If I am going to point my finger and assign blame? I point it directly at us. To the plants who are adapting to the environmental changes we are causing? I extend my gratitude.

I don't miss visiting new worlds across the globe. I no longer feel a need to explore the karri forests of Australia or the volcanic cinders of Hawaii, as enchanting as such places are. I find enough variability in the creatures in our garden and nearby wild places, through time, to keep myself challenged. I like being in tune with my surroundings, though I am simultaneously enthralled and distraught by the changes. I revel in the epic monsoon rains and in the rains falling at "new" times of the year while simultaneously fearing the soaring heat and yearning for constancy and predictability.

No, I don't travel much anymore, but I fly in my imagination to a world where we take responsibility for our actions.

WEATHERING THE CHANGES

SPIDER LILIES: DEFYING THE ODDS

We have babies! Baby Sonoran spider lilies (*Hymenocallis sonorensis*), that is. A small population of this rare Mexican member of the Amaryllis family found her way to our garden after an unusual detour. After being collected by a traveling ethnobotanist, glued to heavy paper, and placed in a sunless ~~mausoleum~~ herbarium, this vouchered specimen defied the odds. She sprouted from her bulb and was noticed (*yay, someone found me!*) and rescued. Once at the home of this same ethnobotanist, she grew more of herself. Some years later, a handful of her offspring was gifted to a like-minded botanical ~~fiend~~ friend, that being me. This year, she produced babies from seeds!

Growing rare or threatened plants is one option for urban gardeners, with appropriate permission, of course.[19] It is not a bad use of water in the city, and co-ordination with other gardeners will help sustain viable populations. At the Phoenix Zoo, if you visit, you may see a small, created stream along which grows a patch of endangered Huachuca water umbel, a tiny plant who looks like a well-manicured lawn for tiny people and whose wetland habitat has been mostly destroyed. Yes, they are growing an endangered plant at the zoo. Mission creep! Another population of this species has been planted at the Desert Botanical Garden. Such urban green spaces educate and engage the public *and* maintain populations of the endangered that someday, maybe, can be used to repopulate the wild once their damaged homes are repaired.

But, you might be wondering, aren't there risks to the plants who grow in cities, too? What if a water pump breaks? What if the reservoir runs dry? Uncertainty is rampant. There are no guarantees that suitable habitat will persist. Our gardening efforts, as well as those of our neighbors, hinge on water that we divert from the big spigot that is the Salt. We pretend that her water is under our control. The dams and reservoirs provide a false sense of security, but we remain at the mercy of external forces.

If we are speculating about the future, what will become of *our* forest garden, should Matt and I no longer be able to tend her? Someday, our bodies and minds will give out. Or we may become climate migrants, like some of our friends. Our forest is only twenty years old. The trees are mere teenagers. Will their

FIGURE 29 Leaves of netleaf hackberry (*Celtis reticulata*). Photo by Matt Chew.

lives be cut short, too? They are just now reaching the level of maturity that attracts old-growth riparian birds such as Lucy's warbler. Seedlings of the shade-tolerant net-leaf hackberry (*Celtis reticulata*), one of my favorite trees, are just now beginning to establish in the understory.

Some urban landholders, who have given this more thought than I, are placing their gardens or farms under the protective umbrellas of conservation easements. They are stipulating that the intent of the gardener be followed after they hand over the reins. I can't bear the thought of leaving our beloveds in the care of someone's non-verdant thumb, yet those are the risks of putting down roots.

All life is temporary. All is in flux. The endangered willow flycatchers who touch down briefly in our oasis while on their migratory journey live but a few years. The spider lilies may persist for a decade or two, the mesquites may live for centuries, and the creosote may persist for millennia. Human societies come and go, done in by the climate or by greed, leaving traces for newcomers to find. Disruption and change are ongoing, and few live to their maximum potential age. All we can do is keep an eye on the uncertainties, make wise choices, and hope to defy the odds.

But to get back to the main point . . . we have babies!

SHIFTING BASELINES

We live near Baseline Road. This very straight street is so named because it tracks the east-west baseline for Arizona as drawn by public land surveyors in 1851. This street reminds me of a concept I discussed with students of restoration ecology, a concept that has its own syndrome: shifting baseline syndrome.[20] Without knowledge of the past—without a sense of historical conditions—each new generation treats the current condition as *normal*. This static and constrained view can lead to pessimism about the *potential* of an ecosystem, thereby limiting our hope and our actions. It also can lead to overoptimism, which carries its own set of risks.

My father was a historian, and I am married to one. I understand how important it is to look back and see where we came from, as a measure of how far we have to go. While those surveyors were surveying, in the mid-1800s, the land on which Matt and I now reside had yet to be plowed. Shrubs such as desert saltbush and creosote peppered her soil and small legume trees lined her ephemeral streams. Not far to the north, the Salt River roamed wildly, undammed, in a floodplain that was miles wide. She was replete with marshes and ponds and the beavers who created them as well as with riparian shrubland, grasslands, and forests. The Piipaash and Akimel O'odham people who relied on her bounty were busily "coaxing food from the desert" by clearing irrigation canals, repairing brush dams (more piles!), and planting tepary beans (*Phaseolus acutifolius*), maize, and squash, "starvation . . . always on the minds of tribal elders."[21] Across the ocean, two of my great-great-grandparents, Sven and Anna Palmquist, following crop failures in Kalmar County, Sweden, were preparing to migrate to a new land where they would begin life anew as plowers of the prairie. Their older boys, including Almond, would attend school, while daughter Augusta stayed home to keep house.

A century after that? By the mid-1900s? The land bordering the Salt River had been plowed and irrigated. Homeowners across the country were growing victory gardens to feed themselves and help the war effort, even if accidentally poisoning the soil with arsenic and other toxins in a misguided effort to kill pests.[22] Farmlands in the Valley were being converted into houses and driveways as post-war growth fueled highways, cars, and urban sprawl. The Salt River had shriveled to a fraction of her former self, being multiply dammed and diverted into canals to feed mostly single-crop fields and single-grass lawns. Baseline Road, in the post-World War II era, was a patchwork of scent-laden color, owing to tenacity of Japanese American flower farmers who persisted, for a while, despite being forcibly removed from their land into encampments. Societies protecting wildflowers were transforming into ones which protected only natives, deepening the divide between humans and nature. I was born into a world in which women were valued mainly for their capacity to procreate and obey but in which Nancy Drews were breaking out of their molds to become independent and strong.

My reality right now? As we careen toward the mid-2000s? I am feeling like it is time to get on with it. The healing. The respect. The living within our means. The widening of our circle of compassion. The recognition that changes need to be made in the way we live on the land. The reverence for the life force—the anima—of which we *all* are a part. The embracement of the Latin *viriditas*—the lush, green, spiritual, and physical health envisioned by the polymath botanist Hildegard, nearly a thousand years ago.

I love finding anecdotal evidence of such a shift. A neighbor down the way, who sells desert trees to those adding canopy to shield us from the increasing heat, is paying homage to Baseline's floral past by planting rows of flowers around their garden. Teachers at local elementary schools are seeking, and receiving, permission to grow food gardens and pollinator gardens and to allow the kids to eat what they grow. Tribal members are teaching others how to grow food in the desert. Friends are asking for help in transforming their patch of compacted soil to a lush and diverse garden, and groups like the Desert Seed Resource Center are organizing to assist them in their endeavors. Forward-looking landscapers like my friend Carianne are envisioning victory climate gardens, to mitigate the escalating extremes.[23] People are thirsty for a new way of being.

With over half of us now living in cities, urban gardeners can have major collective effect. The potential is high. Let's revisit that baseline and embrace a *new* normal.

LINELEAF WHITEPUFF: BEING RESILIENT

Resilience. This is a concept that resonates within the world of ecology and the world of human psychology. Are you more able than some to bounce back from the occasional setback in life? Ecosystems, too, vary in capacity to remain unchanged by external forces *and* in capacity to return to some semblance of starting conditions

FIGURE 30 Lineleaf whitepuff (*Oligomeris linifolia*) in a corner of the garden. Seeds inset in lower left. Photo by Julie Stromberg.

once a stress or disturbance has ceased. Our patch of land has changed dramatically over the years, in response to the plowing, planting, fertilizing, trampling, watering, and not watering, as well as to the rising heat and deposition of air-borne nitrogen that comes with fossil-fueled living.[24] Did any part of "her" remain?

I will answer that question with a name. Lineleaf whitepuff (*Oligomeris linearis*). Despite all the perturbations, despite the frenzied activity of human animals, this tiny winter annual, one wet spring, emerged from the soil seed bank in our dry southwest corner. Not just one. An entire population. She was here all along. Who knows how long she had been waiting, in seed form. Matt and I were thrilled by her presence *and* by her backstory.

It is deeply exciting to have a link to the past residing in a corner of the garden. I have lived in the Southwest for only forty years and my ancestors have been on this continent for only a few hundred. I feel like a nomad, without deep temporal roots. Meeting a small creature whose ancestors have been here for thousands of years, persisting in seed form through megadroughts, gives me needed perspective.

As to her backstory? Most members of lineleaf whitepuff's family—the *Resedaceae*—live in what some call the Old World. Botanists had wondered about this North American disjunct: "The status of the American populations has been obscure, with some authors considering the populations to be introduced, whereas others believe them to be native."[25] The scientists concluded, after molecular genetic sleuthing, that a long-distance dispersal event, during the Quaternary, had carried her from African or Asian deserts to southwestern North America. The genetic evidence did not support a recent anthropogenic introduction. The arrival of this disjunct seed, some thousands of years ago, was declared natural. She was allowed to belong.

Whether lineleaf whitepuff traveled across the globe on the feather of a bird or on a ship with our ancestors, her *belonging* is not in question to me. A dispersal event is a dispersal event, no matter the details. Humans are part of the ecosystem. It is nice to have deep temporal roots, but whatever our tangled history, we are all family.

Indigenous scholar Dr. Jessica Hernandez has a viewpoint that resonates.[26] She suggests that we view plants whose arrival to North America was post-Columbian not as aliens to be maligned but as "displaced relatives" to be respected. She encourages us to set aside our biases and rekindle relationships with *all* plants, no matter whose ancestors they tagged along with. I like that. We are all of this Earth.

I hope the newcomers to the gardening-for-wildlife world or the gardening-for-climate world can resist the external forces who are creating *undue* panic about so-called exotic, alien, or non-native species.[27] If we are to be resilient? We need a large family to rely on. We need many voices to listen to.

CONCLUSION

"IF WE plant it, will they come?" we asked, after moving to a patch of irrigated land near the floodplain of the mighty Salt River in South Phoenix. Yes, they did. Twenty years in, as the vegetation matures and the climate continues its dance, wild birds, insects, reptiles, mammals, and plants continue to arrive to our four-acre garden, with some staying around to make more of themselves. Cultivated ones continue to arrive too; "native" plant sales are hard to resist. Our riparian forest, even if not deep-rooted herself—the groundwater remains beyond reach, pays homage to those with deep ancestral roots in the region while respecting the biocultural heritage of our city. It is satisfying to boost populations of the riparian denizens who once grew wild on the floodplain and terraces before the river was dammed, diverted, and channelized, while also welcoming newcomers who journeyed with humans around the globe.

The inhabitants of the green spaces in our soil-rich neighborhood (Rillito loam!) are as diverse as the animals who tend them. Our rambunctious garden is wilder than most, with its comingling of companions and wildings. We are but one option, but this is our story, and I shall sing its praises as loudly as the cardinals and grackles do. I love being surrounded by bird-filled, aromatic, and climbable trees. My spirits are kept high by the seasonally changing palette of pollinator-laden shrubs and herbaceous perennials. Foraging in our forest on the same foods that Indigenous people have been eating for millennia, and watching our dogs do the same, deepens my attachment to place. I love feeling connected to the patches around me by wind, birds, and other conveyers of seed. I love being aware that I am part of a greater ecosystem, replete with primary producers, consumers, and decomposers. It is empowering to know, and respect, the source of the water that sustains us.

Two decades is not a long time in the scheme of things, but two decades of urban riparian gardening have given me new perspective. I have gained a deeper understanding of resilience, by witnessing the capacity of a tract of land to revitalize as riparian oasis after being plowed, planted to citrus, and abandoned—those lineleaf whitepuffs from the seed bank, and the others who were here all along—what a thrill. I have revitalized a part of me which became buried during my years as scientist: what joy to interact with individual plants as friends after decades of analyzing patterns and traits of the species in which they are placed. I have widened my circle of compassion (I really like flies, now!), and I have restored my hope for the future by witnessing, daily, the tenacity and bounty of life. There is a flip side. By witnessing the struggles of the birds and insects in the increasingly hot environment, I am even more concerned about the future. I am even more committed to reducing my carbon footprint and following a sustainable path.

It is deeply satisfying to be part of a network of urban gardeners who collectively are helping to sustain wildlife, buffer the climate, create beauty, raise moods, and ease pressure on agricultural systems, but I wish there were more of us. If you wish to "plug in" to this green network, and reawaken your inner ecologist, there are many resources available. Volunteer at a community garden, pick up a book on agroecology at your library, attend a class in botany at a local college, or consult with a plant ecologist about growing a victory climate garden. If that seems too much, then simply go outside and observe and listen to the life around you. If your gardening fingers *do* spring to life, let me suggest three maxims to guide you:

First, a messy garden is a biodiverse garden. If you leave dead matter on the ground (piles, yay!), lock the mower in the shed, and let the plants reseed where they like, you may offend a neighbor's sensibility—the pull for clean lines is strong—but the mason bees (*Osmia* spp.) will thank you for their new condominium (plant stems make great bee homes). I understand that relinquishing control can be difficult. But gardening outside of the lines is remarkably freeing. It is a joy to embrace your wildness, and theirs, too.

Second, an inclusive garden is a respectful garden. If you embrace all the wild plants, irrespective of their "nationality," you may offend the members of your local native plant society—nostalgia is a powerful force—but the birds will thank you for the *smörgåsbord*. You will be ahead of your time: distrust and dislike of plants who came from elsewhere are fast becoming a quaint anachronism in these rapidly changing times.

Third, a multi-functional garden is a rewarding garden. A bed of flowers can delight your eyes while also feeding the butterflies. A small woodland in your backyard can deliver a snack while also keeping you cool. The sod of a neighborhood park can sustain busy feet while being bordered by climbable trees. Single-purpose gardening, such as landscaping *just* for aesthetics, is a luxury we no longer can afford.

Whatever type of ecosystem you cocreate will likely be an improvement on the aesthetic of control that dominates many an urban landscape, in public and private spaces alike. "Present day landscapes in Phoenix are designed with a bias toward aesthetical cultural services," says one researcher, leading to a decline in "habitat functions and landscape resilience."[1] The end time is nearing, I hope, for dousing of annual plants with herbicides (they only live a few weeks, what's the problem?), decimating every scrap of organic debris and the insect life it contains with noisy leaf blowers, and pruning plants into submission in the name of beauty.

When I see a crew of landscapers pour out of a van, noisy power tools in their (mostly) male hands, my mind leaps across the taxonomic divide to others who have been controlled. The mindset of control has broad reach in our territorial species. Flowers, like women, are more than pretty "faces." They, like us, are not here just to be looked at. They have work to do. Each generation looks back, aghast, at the unconscionable acts of their grandparents who were behaving within the cultural constraints of their era. I wonder, will our grandchildren look back at our disrespectful treatment of plants—our lack of awareness of their sentience, intelligence, and functional importance—and ask, *how could someone do such a thing?*

How indeed. Ladies and gentlemen, and all those in between: start your (diverse, respectful, and rewarding) gardens.

NOTES

Introduction

1. N. Grimm and S. Schindler, "Nature of Cities and Nature in Cities: Prospects for Conservation and Design of Urban Nature in Human Habitat," in *Rethinking Environmentalism: Linking Justice, Sustainability, and Diversity*, ed. S. Lele, E. S. Brondizio, J. Byrne, G. M. Mace, and J. Martinez-Alier, 99–125 (Cambridge: MIT Press) 2018.
2. S. M. Stroud, S. M. Fennell, J. Mitchley, S. Lydon, J. Peacock, and K. L. Bacon, "The Botanical Education Extinction and the Fall of Plant Awareness," *Ecology and Evolution* 12 (2022): 9019.
3. K. McKenzie, A. Murray, and T. Booth, "Do Urban Environments Increase the Risk of Anxiety, Depression and Psychosis? An Epidemiological Study," *Journal of Affective Disorders* 150 (2013): 1019–1024.

Chapter 1

1. C. M. Levine and J. C. Stromberg, "Effects of Flooding on Native and Exotic Plant Seedlings: Implications for Restoring Southwestern Riparian Forests by Manipulating Water and Sediment Flows," *Journal of Arid Environments* 49 (2001): 111–131.
2. A. Céline, G. M. Luque, and F. Courchamp, "The Twenty Most Charismatic Species," *PLOS One* 13 (2018): 0199149.
3. J. Hecht and A. Horowitz, "Seeing Dogs: Human Preferences for Dog Physical Attributes," *Anthrozoös* 28 (2015): 153–163.

4. J. Blake-Mahmud and L. Struwe, "Time for a Change: Patterns of Sex Expression, Health and Mortality in a Sex-changing Tree," *Annals of Botany* 124 (2019): 367–377.

5. L. J. McGrath and C. van Riper, "Influence of Riparian Tree Phenology on Lower Colorado River Spring-migrating Birds: Implications of Flower Cueing," *U.S. Geological Survey Open-file Report* (2005): 1140.

6. A. L. Rea, *Wings in the Desert: A Folk Ornithology of the Northern Pimans* (Tucson: University of Arizona Press), 2007.

7. W. L. Graf, J. Stromberg, and B. Valentine, "Rivers, Dams, and Willow Flycatchers: a Summary of their Science and Policy Connections," *Geomorphology* 47 (2002):169–188.

8. W. L. Graf, "Locational Probability for a Dammed, Urbanizing Stream: Salt River, Arizona, USA," *Environmental Management* 25 (2000): 321–335.

9. E. Douglas, "Arizona's First Irrigators," *Arizona Highways* (1938): 10 and 25–27.

10. D. Jacobs and S. E. Ingram, "Vegetation Map of Phoenix, Arizona, 1867–1868," *Central Arizona—Phoenix Long-Term Ecological Research Contribution* 3 (2003). J. C. Stromberg, A. Eyden, R. Madera, J. Samsky III, E. Makings, et al., "Provincial and Cosmopolitan: Floristic Composition of a Dryland Urban River," *Urban Ecosystems* 19 (2016): 429–453.

11. J. B. Judd, J. M. Laughlin, H. R. Guenther, and R. Handergrade, "The Lethal Decline of Mesquite on the Casa Grande National Monument," *Great Basin Naturalist* 31 (1971): 153–159.

12. A. Middel, N. Chhetri, and R. Quay, "Urban Forestry and Cool Roofs: Assessment of Heat Mitigation Strategies in Phoenix Residential Neighborhoods," *Urban Forestry & Urban Greening* 14 (2015): 178–186.

13. M. A. Palmer, E. S. Bernhardt, J. D. Allan, P. S. Lake, G. Alexander, et al., "Standards for Ecologically Successful River Restoration," *Journal of Applied Ecology* 42 (2005): 208–217.

14. H. L. Bateman, J. C. Stromberg, M. J. Banville, E. Makings, B. D. Scott, et al., "Novel Water Sources Restore Plant and Animal Communities along an Urban River," *Ecohydrology* 8 (2015): 792–811.

15. J. S. Walker and J. M. Briggs, "An Object-oriented Approach to Urban Forest Mapping in Phoenix," *Programmetric Engineering & Remote Sensing* 5 (2007): 577–583. K. Crewe, "Arizona Native Plants and the Urban Challenge," *Landscape Journal* 32 (2013): 215–229.

Chapter 2

1. C. B. Hensley, C. H. Trisos, P. S. Warren, J. MacFarland, S. C. Blumenshine, et al., "Effects of Urbanization on Native Bird Species in Three Southwestern US Cities," *Frontiers in Ecology and Evolution* 7 (2019): 71.

2. J. F. Chace and J. J. Walsh, "Urban Effects on Native Avifauna: a Review," *Landscape and Urban Planning* 74 (2006): 46–69.

3. E. Nemeth and H. Brumm, "Blackbirds Sing Higher-pitched Songs in Cities: Adaptation to Habitat Acoustics or Side-effect of Urbanization?," *Animal Behaviour* 78 (2009): 637–641.

4. E. H. Strasser and J. A. Heath, "Reproductive Failure of a Human-tolerant Species, the American Kestrel, is Associated with Stress and Human Disturbance," *Journal of Applied Ecology* 5 (2013): 912–919.

5. G. E. Walsberg, "Digestive Adaptations of *Phainopepla nitens* Associated with the Eating of Mistletoe Berries," *The Condor* 77 (1975): 169–174.

6. Portions of this section first appeared in "She Loves Me, She Loves Me Not," an essay written for the City Creatures Blog, a publication of the Center for Humans and Nature, on August 24th, 2021, and is reprinted here with permission of the Center for Humans and Nature Press.

7. D. L. Venable and D. A. Levin, "Ecology of Achene Dimorphism in *Heterotheca latifolia*: I. Achene Structure, Germination and Dispersal," *Journal of Ecology* 73 (1985): 133–145.

8. J. C. Stromberg and D. M Merritt, "Riparian Plant Guilds of Ephemeral, Intermittent and Perennial Rivers," *Freshwater Biology* 8 (2016): 1259–1275.

9. J. A. Boudell and J. C. Stromberg, "Propagule Banks: Potential Contribution to Restoration of an Impounded and Dewatered Riparian Ecosystem," *Wetlands* 28 (2008): 656–665.

10. Portions of this section first appeared in "In Defense of the Immigrant," an essay written for the Earth Island Journal, a publication of the Earth Island Institute, on February 7th, 2022, and is reprinted here with permission of the Earth Island Journal.

11. S. Knapp, L. Dinsmore, C. Fissore, S. E. Hobbie, I. Jakobsdottir, et al., "Phylogenetic and Functional Characteristics of Household Yard Floras and their Changes along an Urbanization Gradient," *Ecology* 93 (2012): S83-S98.

J. S. Walker, N. B. Grimm, J. M. Briggs, C. Gries, and L. Dugan, "Effects of urbanization on plant species diversity in central Arizona," *Frontiers in Ecology and the Environment* 7 (2009): 465–470.

12. M. K. Chew and A. L. Hamilton, "The Rise and Fall of Biotic Nativeness: a Historical Perspective" in *Fifty Years of Invasion Ecology: the Legacy of Charles Elton*, ed. D. M. Richardson, 35–47 (New York: Wiley), 2010.

13. M. A. Davis, "Biotic Globalization: Does Competition from Introduced Species Threaten Biodiversity?," *BioScience* 53 (2003): 481–489.

14. J. C. Stromberg, M. K. Chew, P. L. Nagler, and E. P. Glenn, "Changing Perceptions of Change: the Role of Scientists in *Tamarix* and River Management," *Restoration Ecology* 17 (2009): 177–186.

15. A. G. Tansley, "The Use and Abuse of Vegetational Terms and Concepts," *Ecology* 16 (1935): 284–307.

16. D. Boltovskoy, R. Guiaşu, L. Burlakova, A. Karatayev, M. A. Schlaepfer, and N. Correa, "Misleading Estimates of Economic Impacts of Biological Invasions: Including the Costs but Not the Benefits," *Ambio* 51 (2022): 1786–1799.

17. J. Ollerton, S. Watts, S. Connerty, J. Lock, L. Parker, et al., "Pollination Ecology of the Invasive Tree Tobacco *Nicotiana glauca*: Comparisons across Native and Non-native Ranges," *Journal of Pollination Ecology* 9 (2012): 85–95.

18. C. D. Thomas, "Local Diversity Stays about the Same, Regional Diversity Increases, and Global Diversity Declines," *Proceedings of the National Academy of Sciences* 110 (2013): 19187–19188.

19. M. K. Chew, "Ecologists, Environmentalists, Experts, and the Invasion of the 'Second Greatest Threat,'" *International Review of Environmental History* 1 (2015): 7–40.

    M. A. Dueñas, H. J. Rufhead, N. H. Wakefeld. P. D. Roberts, D. J. Hemming, and H. Diaz-Solter. "The Role Played by Invasive Species in Interactions with Endangered and Threatened Species in the United States: a Systematic Review," *Biodiversity and Conservation* 27 (2018): 3171–3183.

20. T. J. Stohlgren, D. T. Barnett, C. S. Jarnevich, C. Flather, and J. Kartesz, "The Myth of Plant Species Saturation," *Ecology Letters* 11 (2008): 313–322.

21. P. E. Gibbs and S. Talavera, "Breeding System Studies with Three Species of *Anagallis* (*Primulaceae*): Self-incompatibility and Reduced Female Fertility in *A. monelli* L.," *Annals of Botany* 88 (2001): 139–144.

22. P. Del Tradici, "Spontaneous Urban Vegetation: Reflections of Change in a Globalized World," *Nature and Culture* 5 (2010): 299–315.

Chapter 3

1. S. L. Buchmann, G. P. Nabhan, and P. Mirocha, *The Forgotten Pollinators* (Washington, D. C: Island Press), 1996.

2. M. M. López-Uribe, J. H. Cane, R. L. Minckley, and B. N. Danforth, "Crop Domestication Facilitated Rapid Geographical Expansion of a Specialist Pollinator, the Squash Bee *Peponapis pruinosa*," *Proceedings of the Royal Society B* 283 (2016): 20160443.

3. J. E. Bowers, "Has Climatic Warming Altered Spring Flowering Date of Sonoran Desert Shrubs?," *The Southwestern Naturalist* 52 (2007): 347–355.

4. B. N. Danforth, R. L. Minckley, J. L. Neff, and F. Fawcett, *The Solitary Bees—Biology, Evolution, Conservation* (Princeton: Princeton University Press), 2019.

5. S. E. Diamond, E. G. Prileson, and R. A. Martin, "Adaptation to Urban Environments," *Current Opinion in Insect Science* 51 (2022): 100893.

6. J. S. Wilson and O. M. Carril, *The Bees in Your Backyard: a Guide to North America's Bees* (Princeton: Princeton University Press), 2015.

7. F. S. Chew and R. K. Robbins, "Egg-laying in Butterflies," in *The Biology of Butterflies*, ed. R. I. Vane-Wright and P. R. Ackery, 65–79 (London: Academic Press), 1984.

8. C. M. Penz and H. W. Krenn, "Behavioral Adaptations to Pollen-feeding in *Heliconius* Butterflies (*Nymphalidae, Heliconiinae*): an Experiment using Lantana Flowers," *Journal of Insect Behavior* 13 (2000): 865–880.

9. K. R. Nail, L. Drizd, and K. J. Voorhies, "Butterflies Across the Globe: a Synthesis of the Current Status and Characteristics of Monarch (*Danaus*

plexippus) Populations Worldwide," *Frontiers in Ecology and Evolution* 7 (2019): 362.

10. S. E. Diamond and R. A. Martin, "Evolution in Cities," *Annual Review of Ecology, Evolution, and Systematics* 52 (2021): 519–540.

11. A. M. Shapiro, "The Californian Urban Butterfly Fauna is Dependent on Alien Plants," *Diversity and Distributions* 8 (2002): 31–40.

12. C. Fontaine, I. Dajoz, J. Meriguet, and M. Loreau, "Functional Diversity of Plant–pollinator Interaction Webs Enhances the Persistence of Plant Communities," *PLOS Biology* 4 (2006): 1.
    J. Memmott, "The Structure of a Plant-Pollinator Food Web," Ecology Letters 2 (1999): 276–280.

13. Whittaker, D. J., *The Secret Perfume of Birds: Uncovering the Science of Avian Scent* (Baltimore: Johns Hopkins University Press), 2022.

Chapter 4

1. A. Fleming 2020, "More Birds and Bees, Please! 12 Easy, Expert Ways to Rewild Your Garden," *The Guardian* (2020), https://www.theguardian.com/lifeandstyle/2020/may/12/more-birds-and-bees-please-12-easy-expert-ways-to-rewild-your-garden.

2. P. J. Hudson, A. P. Dobson, and K. D. Lafferty, "Is a Healthy Ecosystem One that is Rich in Parasites?," *Trends in Ecology and Evolution* 21 (2006): 381–385.

3. M. Šimpraga, J. Takabayashi, and J. K. Holopainen, "Language of Plants: Where is the Word?," *Journal of Integrative Plant Biology* 58 (2016): 343–349.
   J. E. Dombrowski and R. C. Martin, "Activation of MAP Kinases by Green Leaf Volatiles in Grasses," *BMC Research Notes* 11 (2018): 79.

4. A. Kimbrell, *Fatal Harvest: The Tragedy of Industrial Agriculture* (Washington, D. C.: Island Press), 2002.

5. K. Martin, "The Price of Anything Is the Amount of Life You Exchange for It," *Thoreau Farm* (2017), https://thoreaufarm.org/2017/02/the-price-of-anything-is-the-amount-of-life-you-exchange-for-it.

Chapter 5

1. F. Galibert, P. Quignon, C. Hitte, and C. André, "Toward Understanding Dog Evolutionary and Domestication History," *Comptes Rendus Biologies* 334 (2011): 190–196.

2. B. Kingsolver, *Animal, Vegetable, Mineral: a Year of Food Life* (New York: HarperCollins), 2007.

3. D. O'Brien, *Wild Idea: Buffalo and Family in a Difficult Land* (Lincoln: University of Nebraska Press), 2014.

4. J. W. Hody and R. Kays, "Mapping the Expansion of Coyotes (*Canis latrans*) across North and Central America," *ZooKeys* 759 (2018): 81–97.

M. Grinder and P. R. Krausman, "Morbidity-mortality Factors and Survival of an Urban Coyote Population in Arizona," *Journal of Wildlife Disease* 37 (2001): 312–317.

5. J. A. Foley, C. Monfreda, N. Ramankutty, and D. Zak, "Our Share of the Planetary Pie," *Proceedings of the National Academy of Sciences* 104 (2007): 12585–12586.

6. C. Vörösmarty, D. Lettenmaier, C. Leveque, M. Meybeck, C. Pahl-Wostl, et al., "Humans Transforming the Global Water System," *EOS* 85 (2004): 509–520.

7. N. Kronfeld-Schor and T. Dayan, "Partitioning of Time as an Ecological Resource," *Annual Review of Ecology, Evolution, and Systematics* 34 (2003): 153–181.

8. W. S. Phillips, "Depth of Roots in Soil," *Ecology* 44 (1963): 424.

9. J. C. Stromberg, "Root Patterns and Hydrogeomorphic Niches of Riparian Plants in the American Southwest," *Journal of Arid Environments* 94 (2013): 1–9.

10. J. L. Horton and S. C. Hart, "Hydraulic Lift: a Potentially Important Ecosystem Process," *Trends in Ecology and Evolution* 13 (1998): 232–235.

11. M. Gagliano, M. Grimonprez, M. Depczynski, and M. Renton, "Tuned In: Plant Roots Use Sound to Locate Water," *Oecologia* 18 (2017): 151–160.

12. P. W. Rundel, E. T. Nilsen, M. R. Sharifi, R. A. Virginia, W. M. Jarrell, et al., "Seasonal Dynamics of Nitrogen Cycling for a *Prosopis* Woodland in the Sonoran Desert," *Plant and Soil* 67 (1982): 343–353.

13. P. Felker, "Mesquite Flour: New Life for an Ancient Staple," *Gastronomica* 5 (2005): 85–89.

14. G. Nabhan, *Mesquite—An Arboreal Love Affair* (White River Junction: Chelsea Green Publishing, 2018).

15. W. C. Hodgson, *Food Plants of the Sonoran Desert* (Tucson: University of Arizona Press), 2001.

16. S. C. Anderson, P. R Elsen, B. B. Hughes, R. K. Tonietto, M. C. Bletz, et al., "Trends in Ecology and Conservation over Eight Decades," *Frontiers in Ecology and the Environment* 19 (2021): 274–282.

17. E. Salmón, *Eating the Landscape: American Indian Stories of Food, Identity, and Resilience* (Tucson: University of Arizona Press), 2012.

18. W. H. Drury, Jr., *Chance and Change: Ecology for Conservationists* (Berkeley: University of California Press), 1998.

Chapter 6

1. R. K. Zarger and J. R. Stepp, "Persistence of Botanical Knowledge among Tzeltal Maya Children," *Current Anthropology* 45 (2004): 413–418.

2. A. Balmford, L. Clegg, T. Coulson, and J. Taylor, "Why Conservationists Should Heed Pokémon," *Science* 295 (2002): 2367.

3. S. Kesebir and P. Kesebir, "A Growing Disconnection from Nature is Evident in Cultural Products," *Perspectives on Psychological Science* 12 (2017): 258–269.

4. S. Lui, R. Costanza, S. Farber, and A. Troy, "Valuing Ecosystem Services: Theory, Practice, and the Need for a Transdisciplinary Synthesis," *Annals of the New York Academy of Sciences* 1185 (2010): 54–78.

5. L. Simcha, "How Monocarpic is Agave?," *Flora* 230 (2017): 12–13.
6. South African National Biodiversity Institute. *"Agave americana," PlantzAfrica* (undated), https://pza.sanbi.org/Agave-americana/.
7. C. Diller, M. Castañeda-Zárate, and S. D. Johnson, "Generalist Birds Outperform Specialist Sunbirds as Pollinators of an African Aloe," *Biology Letters* 15 (2019): 20190349.
8. P. Chithra, G. B. Sajithlal, and G. Chandrakasan, "Influence of *Aloe vera* on Collagen Characteristics in Healing Dermal Wounds in Rats," *Molecular and Cellular Biochemistry* 181 (1998): 71–76.
9. K. C. Parker, D. W Trapnell, J. L. Hamrick, W. C. Hodgson, and A. J Parker, "Inferring Ancient Agave Cultivation Practices from Contemporary Genetic Patterns," *Molecular Ecology* 19 (2010): 1622–1637.
10. W. C. Hodgson, *Food Plants of the Sonoran Desert* (Tucson: University of Arizona Press), 2001.
11. T. Izawa, "What is Going on with the Hormonal Control of Flowering in Plants?," *The Plant Journal* 105 (2021): 431–445.
12. S. E. Donnelly, C. J. Lortie, and L. W. Aarssen, "Pollination in *Verbascum thapsus (Scrophulariaceae)*: the Advantage of Being Tall," *American Journal of Botany* 85 (1998): 1618–1625.

Chapter 7

1. M. P. Griffith, "The Origins of an Important Cactus Crop, *Opuntia ficus-indica* (Cactaceae): New Molecular Evidence," *American Journal of Botany* 91 (2004): 1915–1921.
2. J. H. Skevington and P. T. Dang, "Exploring the Diversity of Flies (Diptera)," *Biodiversity* 3 (2011): 3–27.
3. B. M. H. Larson, P.G. Kevan, and D. W. Inouye, "Flies and Flowers: Taxonomic Diversity of Anthophiles and Pollinators," *The Canadian Entomologist* 133 (2012): 439–465.
4. A. P. Martínez-Falcón, M.Á. Marcos-García, C. E. Moreno, and G. E. Rotheray, "A Critical Role for *Copestylum* Larvae (Diptera, Syrphidae) in the Decomposition of Cactus Forests," *Journal of Arid Environments* 78 (2012): 41–48.
5. S. C. H. Barrett, "Darwin's Legacy: the Forms, Function and Sexual Diversity of Flowers," *Philosophical Transactions of the Royal Society of London B* 365 (2010): 351–368.
6. A. Asatryan and N. Tel-Zur, "Pollen Tube Growth and Self-incompatibility in Three *Ziziphus* Species (Rhamnaceae)," *Flora—Morphology, Distribution, Functional Ecology of Plants* 208 (2013): 390–399.
7. S. Songa, A. W. L. Ee, J. K. N. Tan, J. C. Cheong, Z. Chiam, et al., "Upcycling Food Waste Using Black Soldier Fly Larvae: Effects of Further Composting on Frass Quality, Fertilising Effect and its Global Warming Potential," *Journal of Cleaner Production* 288 (2021): 125664.

8. Y. van der Hoek, G. V. Gaona, and K. Martin, "The Diversity, Distribution and Conservation Status of the Tree-cavity-nesting Birds of the World," *Diversity and Distributions* 23 (2017): 1120–1131.

9. S. Van Wassenbergh, E. J. Ortlieb, M. Mielke, C. Böhmer, R. E. Shadwick, and A. Abourachid, "Woodpeckers Minimize Cranial Absorption of Shocks," *Current Biology* 32 (2022): 3189–3194.

10. A. Pecenko and C. Brack, "Habitat Value Of, and Social Attitudes Towards, Dead Trees in Canberra's Urban Forest," *Australian Forestry* 84 (2021): 1–14.

11. L. Chittka, *The Mind of a Bee* (Princeton: Princeton University Press), 2002. B. Danforth, "Bees," *Current Biology* 17 (2007): R156.

12. M. A. Naranjo-Ortiz and T. Gabaldon, "Fungal Evolution: Diversity, Taxonomy and Phylogeny of the Fungi," *Biological Reviews* 94 (2019): 2101–2137.

13. Y. M. Li, J. P. Shaffer, B. Hall, and H. Ko, "Soil-borne Fungi Influence Seed Germination and Mortality, with Implications for Coexistence of Desert Winter Annual Plants," *PLOS One* 14 (2019): 0224417.

14. J. C. Stutz, V. B. Beauchamp, J. Johnson, L. J. Kennedy, et al., "Mycorrhizal Ecology" in *Ecology and Conservation of the San Pedro River*, ed. J. C. Stromberg and B. Tellman, 73–88 (Tucson: University of Arizona Press), 2009.

15. M. A. Gorzelak, A. K. Asay, B. J. Pickles, and S. W. Simard, "Inter-plant Communication Through Mycorrhizal Networks Mediates Complex Adaptive Behaviour in Plant Communities," *AoB Plants* 7 (2015): plv050.

16. M. Cheek, E.N. Lughadha, P. Kirk, H. Lindon, J. Carretero, et al., "New Scientific Discoveries: Plants and Fungi," *Plants, People, Planet* 2 (2009): 371–388.

17. S. E. Hannula, E. Morriën, M. de Hollander, W. H. van der Putten, J. A. van Veen, and W. de Boer, "Shifts in Rhizosphere Fungal Community During Secondary Succession Following Abandonment From Agriculture," *The ISME Journal* 11 (2017): 2294–2304.

18. N. P. Bhatia, A. Adholeya, and A. Sharma, "Biomass Production and Changes in Soil Productivity During Longterm Cultivation of *Prosopis juliflora* (Swartz) DC Inoculated with VA Mycorrhiza and *Rhizobium* spp. in a Semi-arid Wasteland," *Biology and Fertility of Soils* 26 (1998): 208–214.

19. E. C. Jongman, I. Bidstrup, and P.H. Hemsworth, "Behavioural and Physiological Measures of Welfare of Pregnant Mares Fitted with a Novel Urine Collection Device," *Applied Animal Behaviour Science* 93 (2005): 147–163.

20. M. J. Richardson, "Diversity and Occurrence of Coprophilous Fungi," *Mycological Research* 105 (2001): 387–402.

21. S. T. Tadesse, O. Oenema, C. van Beek, and F. L. Ocho, "Manure Recycling from Urban Livestock Farms for Closing the Urban–Rural Nutrient Loops," *Nutrient Cycling in Agroecosystems* 119 (2021): 51–67.

22. W. G. Whitford, "Subterranean Termites and Long-term Productivity of Desert Rangelands," *Sociobiology* 19 (1991): 235–243. W. G. Whitford and B. D. Duval, *Ecology of Desert Ecosystems*, second edition (Amsterdam: Elsevier Academic Press), 2020.

Chapter 8

1. J. M. Bates, "Frugivory on *Bursera microphylla* (Burseraceae) by Wintering Gray Vireos (*Vireo vicinior*, Vireonidae) in the Coastal Deserts of Sonora, Mexico," *The Southwestern Naturalist* 37 (1992): 252–258.

2. M. Mertens, A. Buettner, and E. Kirchhoff, "The Volatile Constituents of Frankincense—a Review," *Flavour and Fragrance Journal* 24 (2009): 279–300.

3. A. Horowitz, *Inside of a Dog: What Dogs See, Smell and Know* (New York: Simon and Schuster, 2010).

4. A. V. Oliveira-Pinto, R. M. Santos, R. A. Coutinho, L. M. Oliveira, G. B. Santos, et al., "Sexual Dimorphism in the Human Olfactory Bulb: Females Have More Neurons and Glial Cells Than Males," *PLOS One* 9 (2014): 111733.

5. A. Gilbert, *What the Nose Knows: The Science of Scent in Everyday Life* (New York: Crown Publishers), 2014.

6. W. A. Buttemer, L. B Astheimer, and W. W Weathers, "Energy Savings Attending Winter-nest Use by Verdins (*Auriparus flaviceps*)," *The Auk* 104 (1987): 531–535.

7. K. J. Odom, M. L. Hall, K. Riebel, K. E. Omland, and N. E. Langmore, "Female Song is Widespread and Ancestral in Songbirds," *Nature Communications* 5 (2014): 3379.

8. K. Riebel, K. J. Odom, N. E. Langmore, and M. L. Hall, "New Insights From Female Bird Song: Towards an Integrated Approach to Studying Male and Female Communication Roles," *Biology Letters* 15 (2019): 20190059.

9. D. M. Ferraro, Z. D. Miller, L. A. Ferguson, B. D. Taff, J. R. Barber, P. Newman, and C. D. Francis, "The Phantom Chorus: Birdsong Boosts Human Well-being in Protected Areas," *Proceedings of the Royal Society B* 287 (2020): 20201811.

10. Y. Wen, Q. Yan, Y. Pan, X. Gu, and Y. Liu, "Medical Empirical Research on Forest Bathing (Shinrin-yoku): a Systematic Review," *Environmental Health and Preventive Medicine* 24 (2019):1–21.

11. I. Markevych, E. Thiering, E. Fuertes, D. Sugiri, D. Berdel, et al., "A Cross-sectional Analysis of the Effects of Residential Greenness on Blood Pressure in 10-year Old Children: Results from the GINIplus and LISAplus Studies," *BMC Public Health* 14 (2014): 477.

12. C. Hall and M. Knuth, "An Update of the Literature Supporting the Well-being Benefits of Plants: a Review of the Emotional and Mental Health Benefits of Plants," *Journal of Environmental Horticulture* 37 (2019): 30–38.

13. F. Williams, *The Nature Fix: Why Nature Makes Us Happier, Healthier, and More Creative* (New York: W. W. Norton & Company, 2017).

14. L. I. Labrecque and G. R. Milne, "Exciting Red and Competent Blue: the Importance of Color in Marketing," *Journal of the Academy of Marketing Science* 40 (2012): 711–727.

15. K. Takeda, "Blue Metal Complex Pigments Involved in Blue Flower Color," *Proceedings of the Japan Academy, Series B* 82 (2006): 142–54.

16. A. Dance, "The Incredible Diversity of Viruses," *Nature* 595 (2021): 22–25.

17. M. Breitbart and F. Rohwer, "Here a Virus, There a Virus, Everywhere the Same Virus?," *Trends in Microbiology* 13 (2005): 278–284.

18. N. Grand and E. Tramontano, "Human Endogenous Retroviruses are Ancient Acquired Elements Still Shaping Innate Immune Responses," *Frontiers in Immunology* 9 (2018): 2039.

19. G. Benítez, M. March-Salas, A. Villa-Kamel, U. Cháves-Jiménez, J. Hernández, et al., "The Genus *Datura* L. (*Solanaceae*) in Mexico and Spain—Ethnobotanical Perspective at the Interface of Medical and Illicit Uses," *Journal of Ethnopharmacology* 219 (2018): 133–151.

20. H. Guan-Zhu, "Origin and Evolution of the Plant Immune System," *New Phytologist* 222 (2019): 70–83.

21. H. M. Alexander, K. E. Mauck, A. E. Whitfield, K. A. Garrett, and C. M. Malmstrom, "Plant-virus Interactions and the Agro-ecological Interface," *European Journal of Plant Pathology* 138 (2014): 529–547.

22. H. Hamzah, N. Othman, N. Badrulhisham, and L. Karlinasari, "Unintentional Vandalism: Unskilled Tree Pruning Practices in Tree Management," *Landscape and Urban Planning* 207 (2021): 104018.

Chapter 9

1. D. A. Raichlen, A. D. Foster, G. L. Gerdeman, A. Seillier, and A. Giuffrida, "Wired to Run: Exercise-induced Endocannabinoid Signaling in Humans and Cursorial Mammals with Implications for the 'Runner's High,'" *Journal of Experimental Biology* 215 (2012): 1331–1336.

2. J. Sams and D. Carson, *Medicine Cards: the Discovery of Power Through the Ways of Animals* (Rochester: Bear & Company), 1992.

3. R. A. Bradley and S. Buchanan, *Common Spiders of North America* (Berkeley: University of California Press, 2019).

4. T. S. Kraft, V. V. Venkataraman, and N. J. Dominy, "A Natural History of Human Tree Climbing," *Journal of Human Evolution* 71 (2014): 105–11.

5. D. A. Raichlen, B. M. Wood, A. D. Gordon, A. Z. P. Mabulla, F. W. Marlowe, and H. Pontzer, "Evidence of Levy Walk Foraging Patterns in Human Hunter-gatherers," *Proceedings of the National Academy of Sciences* 111 (2013): 728–733.

6. E. Frith, S. Miller, and P. D. Loprinzi, "A Review of Experimental Research on Embodied Creativity: Revisiting the Mind–Body Connection," *Journal of Creative Behavior* 54 (2020): 767–798.

7. S. Silverstein, *Where the Sidewalk Ends* (New York: Harper and Row Publishers), 1974.

8. R. Yabes, K. Shetter, and J. Schneeman, "Urban Waterways: Changing Historical Uses and Users in a Southwestern Desert City," *Landscape and Urban Planning* 39 (1997): 167–185.

9. Y. Yang, D. Tilman, G. Furey, and C. Lehman, "Soil Carbon Sequestration Accelerated by Restoration of Grassland Biodiversity," *Nature Communications* 10 (2019): 718.

10. P. D. Thacker, "California Butterflies: At Home with Aliens," *BioScience* 54 (2004): 182–187.

11. S. Venn and D. Johan, "Benign Neglect Enhances Urban Habitat Heterogeneity: Responses of Vegetation and Carabid Beetles (Coleoptera: *Carabidae*) to the Cessation of Mowing of Park Lawns," *European Journal of Entomology* 111 (2014): 703–714.

12. M. Willburn, "In Defense of Inclusive Biodiversity," *Garden Rant: Uprooting the Garden World* (2021), https://gardenrant.com/2021/04/in-defense-of -inclusive-biodiversity.html.

13. J. O'Keefe, N. Burgess, J. G. Donnett, K. J. Jeffery, and E. A. Maguire, "Place Cells, Navigational Accuracy, and the Human Hippocampus," *Philosophical Transactions of the Royal Society B* 353 (1998): 1333–1340.

14. J. C Stromberg, E. Makings, D. E. Brown, and D. Wolkis, "Conservation of the Cienega Endemic, *Eryngium sparganophyllum* Hemsl. (*Apiaceae*)," *Southwest Naturalist* 65 (2020): 173–184.

15. B. Kaiser, G. Vogg, U. B. Fürst, and M. Albert, "Parasitic Plants of the Genus *Cuscuta* and Their Interaction with Susceptible and Resistant Host Plants," *Frontiers in Plant Science* 6 (2014): 45.

16. J. H. Cota-Sánchez, J. G. O. Almeida, D. J. Falconer, H. J. Choi, and L. Bevan, "Intriguing Thigmonastic (Sensitive) Stamens in the Plains Prickly Pear *Opuntia polyacantha* (*Cactaceae*)," *Flora—Morphology, Distribution, Functional Ecology of Plants* 208 (2013): 381–389.

Chapter 10

1. D. M. Wilkinson and T. N. Sherratt, "Why Is the World Green? The Interactions of Top-Down and Bottom-Up Processes in Terrestrial Vegetation Ecology," *Plant Ecology & Diversity* 9 (2016): 127–140.

2. W. J. Ripple, J. A. Estes, O. J. Schmitz, V. Constant, M. J. Kaylor, et al., "What is a Trophic Cascade?," *Trends in Ecology & Evolution* 31 (2016): 842–849.

3. J. Núñez-Farfán, J. Fornoni, and P. L. Valverde, "The Evolution of Resistance and Tolerance to Herbivores," *Annual Review of Ecology, Evolution, and Systematics* 38 (2007): 541–566.

4. S. Xu, W. Zhou, S. Pottinger, and I. T. Baldwin, "Herbivore Associated Elicitor-induced Defenses are Highly Specific Among Closely Related *Nicotiana* Species," *BMC Plant Biology* 15 (2015): 2.

5. A. A. Agrawal, "Induced Responses to Herbivory and Increased Plant Performance," *Science* 279 (1998): 1201–1202.

6. K. L. Lum, J. R. Polansky, R. K. Jackler, and S. A. Glantz, "Signed, Sealed and Delivered: 'Big Tobacco' in Hollywood, 1927–1951," *Tobacco Control* 17 (2008): 313–323.

7. G. E. Hutchinson, "Homage to Santa Rosalia or Why Are There So Many Kinds of Animals?" *The American Naturalist* 93 (1959): 145–159.

8. P. K. Bretting and G. P. Nabhan, "Ethnobotany of Devil's Claw (*Proboscidea parviflora* ssp. *parviflora: Martyniaceae*) in the Greater Southwest," *Journal of California and Great Basin Anthropology* 8 (1986): 226–237.

9. H. R. Roberts, J. M. Warren, and J. Provan, "Evidence for Facultative Protocarnivory in *Capsella bursa-pastoris* Seeds," *Scientific Reports* 8 (2018): 10120.

10. L. Kubiak-Martens, "The Plant Food Component of the Diet at the Late Mesolithic (Ertebolle) Settlement at Tybrind Vig, Denmark," *Vegetation History and Archaeobotany* 8 (1999): 117–127.

11. D. Curtin, "Making Peace with the Earth: Indigenous Agriculture and the Green Revolution," *Environmental Ethics* 17 (1995): 59–73.
   I. Sobha, "Green Revolution: Impact on Gender," *Journal of Human Ecology* 22 (2007): 107–113.

12. P. Flombaum and O. E. Sala, "Higher Effect of Plant Species Diversity on Productivity in Natural than Artificial Ecosystems," *Proceedings of the National Academy of Science* 105 (2008): 6087–6090.

13. M. A. Altieri, *Agroecology: the Science of Sustainable Agriculture* (Boca Raton: CRC Press), 1995.

14. J. Trujillo-Arriaga and M. A. Altieri, "A Comparison of Aphidophagous Arthropods on Maize Polycultures and Monocultures, in Central Mexico," *Agriculture, Ecosystems & Environment* 31 (1990): 337–349.

15. G. Nabhan, *Food from the Radical Center—Healing Our Land and Communities* (Washington, D. C.: Island Press), 2018.

16. N. Eriksson, S. Wu, C. B. Do, A. K. Kiefer, J. Y Tung, et al., "A Genetic Variant Near Olfactory Receptor Genes Influences Cilantro Preference," *Flavour* 1 (2012): 22.

17. D. J. Herrera, M. V. Cove, W. J. McShea, D. T. Flockhart, S. Decker, et al., "Prey Selection and Predation Behavior of Free-roaming Domestic Cats (*Felis catus*) in an Urban Ecosystem: Implications for Urban Cat Management," *Biological Conservation* 268 (2022): 109503.

18. C. B. Eötvösa, T. Magura, and G. L. Löveic, "A Meta-analysis Indicates Reduced Predation Pressure With Increasing Urbanization," *Landscape and Urban Planning* 180 (2018): 54–59.

19. S. H. Faeth, P. S. Warren, E. Shochat, and W. A. Marussich, "Trophic Dynamics in Urban Communities," *BioScience* 55 (2005): 399–407.

20. R. Dicker, "Fox Runs Amok at Arizona State Football Game and It's Wild," *Huffington Post* (2021), https://www.huffpost.com/entry/fox-arizona-state-football_n_618956e7e4b055e47d7e0eae.

21. M. L. Rosenzweig, *Win-Win Ecology: How the Earth's Species Can Survive in the Midst of Human Enterprise* (New York: Oxford University Press), 2003.

22. Q. S. Zhen, X. Yea, and Z. J. Weiab, "Recent Progress in Research on *Tripterygium*: a Male Antifertility Plant," *Contraception* 51 (1995): 121–129.

23. K. Wiseman, H. W. Greene, M. S. Koo, and D. J. Long, "Feeding Ecology of a Generalist Predator, the California Kingsnake (*Lampropeltis california*): Why Rare Prey Matter," *Herpetological Conservation and Biology* 14 (2019): 1–30.

24. W. A. Wingert and L. Chan, "Rattlesnake Bites in Southern California and Rationale for Recommended Treatment," *Western Journal of Medicine* 148 (1988): 37–44.

Chapter 11

1. G. Garfin, A. Jardine, R. Merideth, M. Black, and S. LeRoy, ed., *Assessment of Climate Change in the Southwest United States* (Washington, D. C.: Island Press), 2013.

2. W. T. L. Chow, D. Brennan, and A. J. Brazel, "Urban Heat Island Research in Phoenix, Arizona: Theoretical Contributions and Policy Applications," *Bulletin of the American Meteorological Society* 93 (2012): 517–530.

3. A. Huddleston, "Happy 200th Birthday to Eunice Foote, Hidden Climate Science Pioneer," *National Oceanic and Atmospheric Administration* (2019), https://www.climate.gov/news-features/features/happy-200th-birthday-eunice-foote-hidden-climate-science-pioneer.

4. F. Molena, "Remarkable Weather of 1911—The Effect of the Combustion of Coal on the Climate—What Scientists Predict for the Future," *Popular Mechanics* 17 (1912): 339–342.

5. C. A. Anderson, "Heat and Violence," *Current Directions in Psychological Science* 10 (2001): 33–38.

6. D. T. Kenrick and S. W. MacFarlane, "Ambient Temperature and Horn Honking: a Field Study of the Heat/Aggression Relationship," *Environment and Behavior* 18 (1986): 179–191.

7. G. B. Anderson, M. L. Bell, and R. D. Peng, "Methods to Calculate the Heat Index as an Exposure Metric in Environmental Health Research," *Environmental Health Perspectives* 121 (2013): 1111–1119.

8. J. R. Nelson, A. Grubesic, J. A. Miller, and A. W. Chamberlain, "The Equity of Tree Distribution in the Most Ruthlessly Hot City in the United States: Phoenix, Arizona," *Urban Forestry & Urban Greening* 59 (2021): 127016.

J. Declet-Barreto, A. J. Brazel, C. A. Martin, W. T. L. Chow, and S. L. Harlan, "Creating the Park Cool Island in an Inner-city Neighborhood: Heat Mitigation Strategy for Phoenix, AZ," *Urban Ecosystems* 16 (2013): 617–635.

9. M. A. Rahmana, L. M. F. Stratopoulos, A. Moser-Reischl, T. Zölcha, K. Häberle, et al., "Traits of Trees for Cooling Urban Heat Islands: a Meta-analysis," *Building and Environment* 170 (2020): 106606.

A. Ordonez and H. Olff, "Do Alien Plant Species Profit More from High Resource Supply than Natives? A Trait-Based Analysis," *Global Ecology and Biogeography* 22 (2012): 648–658.

10. J. M. Marzluff, *Welcome to Subirdia: Sharing our Neighborhood with Wrens, Robins, Woodpeckers, and other Wildlife* (New Haven: Yale University Press, 2014).

11. T. Riis, M. Kelly-Quinn, F. C Aguiar, P. Manolaki, D. Bruno, et al., "Global Overview of Ecosystem Services Provided by Riparian Vegetation," *BioScience* 70 (2020): 501–514.

12. A. W. Driscoll, N. Q. Bitter, D. R. Sandquist, and J. R. Ehleringer, "Multidecadal Records of Intrinsic Water-use Efficiency in the Desert Shrub *Encelia farinosa* Reveal Strong Responses to Climate Change," *Proceedings of the National Academy of Sciences* 117 (2020): 18161–18168.

13. R. C. Brusca, J. F. Wiens, W. M. Meyer, J. Eble, K. Franklin, et al., "Dramatic Response to Climate Change in the Southwest: Robert Whittaker's 1963 Arizona Mountain Plant Transect Revisited," *Ecology and Evolution* 3 (2013): 3307–3319.
    S. Hantson, T. E. Huxman, S. Kimball, J. T. Randerson, and M. L. Goulden, "Warming as a Driver of Vegetation Loss in the Sonoran Desert of California," *JGR Biosciences* 126 (2021): 10.1029/2020JG005942.

14. J. Ewan, R. F. Ewan, and J. Burke, "Building Ecology into the Planning Continuum: Case Study of Desert Land Preservation in Phoenix, Arizona (USA)," *Landscape and Urban Planning* 68 (2004): 53–75.

15. D. R. Sandquist and J. R. Ehleringer, "Population—and Family-level Variation of Brittlebush (*Encelia farinosa, Asteraceae*) Pubescence: its Relation to Drought and Implications for Selection in Variable Environments," *American Journal of Botany* 90 (2003): 1481–1486.

16. J. Bowers, *A Full Life in a Small Place: And Other Essays from a Desert Garden* (Tucson: University of Arizona Press), 1992.

17. J. L. Weiss and J. T. Overpeck, "Is the Sonoran Desert Losing its Cool?," *Global Change Biology* 11 (2005): 2065–2077.

18. M. J. Osland, P. W. Stevens, M. M. Lamont, R. C. Brusca, K. M. Hart, et al., "Tropicalization of Temperate Ecosystems in North America: the Northward Range Expansion of Tropical Organisms in Response to Warming Winter Temperatures," *Global Change Biology* 27 (2021): 3009–3034.

19. M. A. Goddard, A. J. Dougill, and T. G. Benton, "Scaling up From Gardens: Biodiversity Conservation in Urban Environments," *Trends in Ecology and Evolution* 25 (2010): 90–98.

20. M. Soga and K. J. Gaston, "Shifting Baseline Syndrome: Causes, Consequences, and Implications," *Frontiers in Ecology and the Environment* 16 (2018): 222–230.

21. B. Allen, "A'aga Something to Be Told: on O'otham Farming," *Gila River Indian News* (April 11, 2017), https://www.gricnews.org/index.php/grin-articles/2017-articles/april-7-2017-articles/aaga-something-to-be-told-on-ootham-farming.

22. J. Sumner, 2019. *Plants go to War: A Botanical History of World War II* (Jefferson: McFarland & Company Inc.), 2019.

23. M. Clarke, M. Davidson, M. Egerer, E. Anderson, and N. Fouch, "The Underutilized Role of Community Gardens in Improving Cities' Adaptation to Climate Change: A Review," *People, Place & Policy Online* 12 (2018): 241–251.

24. S. M. Decina, L. R. Hutyra, and P. H Templer. "Hotspots of Nitrogen Deposition in the World's Urban Areas: a Global Data Synthesis," *Frontiers in Ecology and the Environment* 18 (2019): 92–100.

25. S. Martín-Bravo, P. Vargas, and M. Luceño. "Is *Oligomeris* (*Resedaceae*) Indigenous to North America? Molecular Evidence for a Natural Colonization from the Old World," *American Journal of Botany* 96 (2009): 507–518.

26. J. Hernandez, *Fresh Banana Leaves: Healing Indigenous Landscapes through Indigenous Science* (Berkeley: North Atlantic Books), 2022.

27. D. F. Sax, M. A. Schlaepfer, and J. D. Olden, "Valuing the Contributions of Non-native Species to People and Nature," Trends in Ecology and Evolution 37 (2022): 1058–1066.

Conclusion

1. C. A. Martin, "Landscape Sustainability in a Sonoran Desert City," *Cities and the Environment* 1 (2008): 5.

INDEX

ABOUT THE AUTHOR

DR. JULIET C. STROMBERG (Professor Emeritus) is a plant ecologist who specialized in wetland and riparian ecosystems of the American Southwest. With over 100 peer-reviewed publications and one co-edited book (*Ecology and Conservation of the San Pedro River*), she contributed knowledge that was applied in restoration and management contexts and used to safeguard valuable ecosystems for future generations. She recently retired from Arizona State University.